# The SUNDAY GOSPELS *for* ADVENT, CHRISTMAS, LENT AND EASTER

# The SUNDAY GOSPELS *for* ADVENT, CHRISTMAS, LENT AND EASTER

*All the Sunday Mass Gospel readings for years A, B and C from the Revised New Jerusalem Bible*

With commentary and guidance for Lectio Divina by
ADRIAN GRAFFY

DARTON·LONGMAN+TODD

This book is dedicated to
Dom Henry Wansbrough,
monk and biblical scholar

First published in Great Britain in 2020 by
Darton, Longman and Todd Ltd
1 Spencer Court
140–142 Wandsworth High Street
London SW18 4JJ

© 2020 Adrian Graffy

Print book ISBN: 978-0-232-53476-4
eBook ISBN: 978-0-232-53477-1

The right of Adrian Graffy to be identified as the Author of this work has been asserted in accordance with the Copyright, Designs and Patents Act 1988.

Bible extracts taken from The Revised New Jerusalem Bible, published and copyright © 2019 by Darton, Longman and Todd and The Crown Publishing Group, a division of Penguin Random House LLC, New York.

Cover and interior illustration image by Kathleen M. Lindsley,
www.ravenpressgallery.co.uk

A catalogue record for this book is available from the British Library.

Designed and produced by Judy Linard
Printed and bound by ScandBook AB, Sweden

# CONTENTS

## ADVENT

### YEAR A
*First Sunday* — 13
*Second Sunday* — 14
*Third Sunday* — 16
*Fourth Sunday* — 17

### YEAR B
*First Sunday* — 19
*Second Sunday* — 20
*Third Sunday* — 22
*Fourth Sunday* — 24

### YEAR C
*First Sunday* — 25
*Second Sunday* — 27
*Third Sunday* — 28
*Fourth Sunday* — 30

## CHRISTMAS

*The Nativity of Our Lord (Christmas Day)* — 35
*Holy Family (Years A, B, C)* — 37
*Mary, Mother of God* — 42
*Second Sunday after Christmas* — 43
*Epiphany* — 46
*Baptism of the Lord (Years A, B, C)* — 47

# LENT

## YEAR A
| | |
|---|---:|
| *First Sunday* | 55 |
| *Second Sunday* | 57 |
| *Third Sunday* | 58 |
| *Fourth Sunday* | 61 |
| *Fifth Sunday* | 64 |
| *Palm Sunday* | 67 |

## YEAR B
| | |
|---|---:|
| *First Sunday* | 75 |
| *Second Sunday* | 76 |
| *Third Sunday* | 78 |
| *Fourth Sunday* | 79 |
| *Fifth Sunday* | 81 |
| *Palm Sunday* | 83 |

## YEAR C
| | |
|---|---:|
| *First Sunday* | 89 |
| *Second Sunday* | 91 |
| *Third Sunday* | 92 |
| *Fourth Sunday* | 94 |
| *Fifth Sunday* | 96 |
| *Palm Sunday* | 97 |

# EASTER

| | |
|---|---:|
| *Easter Sunday* | 107 |

## YEAR A
| | |
|---|---:|
| *Second Sunday* | 108 |
| *Third Sunday* | 110 |
| *Fourth Sunday* | 111 |
| *Fifth Sunday* | 113 |
| *Sixth Sunday* | 115 |
| *Ascension* | 117 |
| *Seventh Sunday* | 118 |

## YEAR B
*Second Sunday* — 120
*Third Sunday* — 122
*Fourth Sunday* — 123
*Fifth Sunday* — 125
*Sixth Sunday* — 126
*Ascension* — 128
*Seventh Sunday* — 130

## YEAR C
*Second Sunday* — 131
*Third Sunday* — 133
*Fourth Sunday* — 135
*Fifth Sunday* — 136
*Sixth Sunday* — 138
*Ascension* — 140
*Seventh Sunday* — 141
*Pentecost Sunday* — 143

# INTRODUCTION

THE LECTIONARY PRODUCED IN the wake of the Second Vatican Council (1962-1965) has been with us now for more than fifty years. It continues to offer a broad selection of readings from all parts of Scripture.

The gospels on Sunday are the most obvious proclamation of the good news of Jesus Christ. Those who carried through the Council's reforms had the brilliant idea of dedicating a year to each of the Synoptic Gospels – Matthew, Mark and Luke – assigned respectively to Years A, B, and C, and of giving John pride of place in the seasons of Lent and Easter. Each gospel is shown to make a unique contribution to the understanding of Christ, and we are able to recognise more keenly the particular accents and interests of the separate evangelists.

These two volumes on the *Sunday Gospels* provide text and commentary on all the gospel readings that occur on Sundays throughout the three-year cycle adopted for the Sunday lectionary. The first volume considers the 'strong' liturgical times: Advent, Christmas, Lent and Easter. The second volume covers all the remaining Sundays, known as 'Sundays in ordinary time' (*per annum*). Included in the second volume are the solemnities and feasts of the Lord which from time to time fall on Sundays, and displace the celebration of numbered Sundays.

It is probably useful to explain the basic 'shape' of the liturgical year. The 'strong' seasons, Advent, Christmas, Lent and Easter, are never displaced. Ordinary Sundays cover the remaining time. Since the date of Easter varies, the block of Sundays of Lent and Easter shifts too. This means that the number of ordinary Sundays between Christmas and Lent changes, as does that of Sundays between Pentecost (the last Sunday of Easter) and Advent.

Years A, B and C usually offer readings from Matthew, Mark and Luke respectively. There are some exceptions to this. For instance, on Sundays 17-21 of Year B (Mark), chapter 6 of the Gospel of John is proclaimed, with its extensive material on the Bread of Life.

How does one work out what year to follow? Each Year begins with Advent but is identified by the numbered year which begins after Christmas. One simply has to add up the four digits in the year, and if they amount to a multiple of three the year will be Year C. Year A is therefore a multiple of three plus one, and Year B a multiple of three plus two. Thus the year 2019 was Year C, because $2 + 0 + 1 + 9$ amount to 12, a multiple of three. Once you have successfully completed the calculation the other Years, of course, follow.

The text of the gospel used here is from the *Revised New Jerusalem Bible*. The work of Dom Henry Wansbrough, this recently published Bible has a freshness and a clarity which is unsurpassed. The scholarship is up-to-date, while the text, clearly written for today's listeners, nevertheless preserves cherished biblical ways of expression, such as 'Blessed are the poor in spirit' and 'Amen, amen I say to you'.

Each gospel text is given in full, and there follows a concise commentary, opening up lines of reflection for individuals and groups, preachers and congregations. The references to all the readings of a given Sunday and to the responsorial psalm are always provided. Each section concludes with two questions and two proposals for prayer, so that the reading becomes both personal and prayerful.

I hope you will find that these volumes provide a gentle and informed companion to the gospel readings offered in the Liturgy of the Word week by week and year by year.

## THE REVD DR ADRIAN GRAFFY

# ADVENT

# YEAR A

## *First Sunday of Advent (Year A)*

### Matthew 24:37-44

Jesus said, 'As it was in Noah's day, so will be the coming of the Son of man. For in those days before the Flood people were eating, drinking, taking wives, taking husbands, until the day Noah went into the ark, and they suspected nothing till the Flood came and swept them all away. So will be the coming of the Son of man. Then of two men in the fields, one is taken, one left; of two women grinding at the mill, one is taken, one left. So stay awake, because you do not know the day when your master is coming.

'You may be sure of this, that if the householder had known at what time of the night the burglar would come, he would have stayed awake and would not have allowed anyone to break through the wall of his house. Therefore, you too must stand ready, because the Son of man is coming at an hour you do not expect.'

**Other readings: Isaiah 2:1-5   Psalm 121 (122)   Romans 13:11-14**

AS A NEW LITURGICAL year begins and the season of Advent starts, it is our tradition to reflect on the final return of Christ, his 'second coming'. During this liturgical year we shall be reading the Gospel of Matthew on Sundays. Towards the end of Matthew's account of the ministry of Jesus, Jesus speaks at length about the future and the end of the world.

Jesus stresses the suddenness and unexpectedness of the end. The fundamental message here is the need to be ready at all times. The day is not known and it is useless for Christians to waste time calculating when the day of Christ's return will come. The message to 'stay awake' is a call to trustful perseverance in generous response to the gospel.

The season of Advent is the time in which we read from the book of the prophet Isaiah, considered by Christians to be the foremost prophet of the Messiah. The invitation to go up to the mountain of the Lord encourages us to continue in faith our Christian journey to God's dwelling place. In due time we will rejoice with the psalmist and say 'and now our feet are standing within your gates, Jerusalem'. Jesus leads us to the city of God. Advent teaches us that we should live our lives in hope and love.

Many Christians have lost the sense of Advent, with the secular 'party season' obscuring its beauty more and more. The beauty of Advent lies in the sure hope that the Lord will come, and in the encouragement of the Scriptures to live the life of faith. In Advent we should examine our Christian response and style of life with honesty and make the changes that faith suggests so that we are indeed always ready to meet the Lord.

*Do I calculate how to reach salvation, or am I constantly ready to welcome the Lord?*
*What changes are required in the way I live the days of Advent and my Christian life?*
*Let us pray for trust, perseverance, and generosity on our journey.*
*Let us pray that the true sense of Advent and Christmas will be rediscovered in our society.*

---

# Second Sunday of Advent (Year A)

## Matthew 3:1–12

In those days, John the Baptist came, proclaiming in the desert of Judaea, saying, 'Repent, for the kingdom of Heaven has drawn near.' This was the man spoken of by the prophet Isaiah when he said:

*A voice of one crying in the desert,*
*'Prepare a way for the Lord,*
*make his paths straight.'*

# SECOND SUNDAY OF ADVENT (YEAR A)    15

John himself wore a garment of camel-hair with a leather belt round his waist, and his food was locusts and wild honey. Then Jerusalem and all Judaea and the whole region around the Jordan district kept going out to him, and they were baptised by him in the River Jordan as they confessed their sins. But seeing many of the Pharisees and Sadducees coming for baptism he said to them, 'Brood of vipers, who warned you to flee from the wrath to come? Produce fruit worthy of repentance, and do not be satisfied with saying to yourselves, "We have Abraham as our father," for I tell you, God can raise children for Abraham from these stones. Even now the axe is being laid to the root of the trees, so any tree failing to produce good fruit is cut down and thrown on the fire. I baptise you with water for repentance, but the one who comes after me is more powerful than I, and I am not fit to carry his sandals; he will baptise you with the Holy Spirit and fire. His winnowing-fan is in his hand; he will clear his threshing-floor and gather his wheat into his barn; but the chaff he will burn in a fire that never goes out.'

**Other readings: Isaiah 11:1-10    Psalm 71 (72)    Romans 15:4-9**

ON THE SECOND SUNDAY of Advent we are introduced to another great Advent figure, John the Baptist. Matthew has him preach, like Jesus, about the coming of the kingdom of heaven. His preaching fulfils the words found in the prophet Isaiah about 'a voice crying in the wilderness'.

John is dressed like a prophet and lives in the wilderness. Those who come to him receive a baptism of repentance for their sins. John fiercely attacks those who have relied on their status and their traditions for their salvation. They have relied on being 'children of Abraham' and have become complacent. For John, the love of God is not limited to the chosen race, and all men and women are called to produce good fruit.

John's principal task is to point to the 'one who comes after me'. This one is more powerful and will bring a new baptism, in the Holy Spirit. With the preaching of John the Baptist, the liturgy is preparing us for the coming of Christ.

*Do I listen out for the voice of the prophet crying in the wilderness of this world?*

*Do I rely on my 'status' as a Christian rather than striving to live as one?*

*Let us pray for true repentance, and for courage in living and proclaiming God's good news.*

*Let us pray for a deeper reverence and love for the Holy Scriptures.*

---

# *Third Sunday of Advent (Year A)*

## *Matthew 11:2–11*

Now John had heard in prison what the Messiah was doing and he sent his disciples to ask him, 'Are you the one who is to come, or are we to expect someone else?' Jesus answered, 'Go back and tell John what you hear and see; the blind see again, and the lame walk, lepers are cleansed, and the deaf hear, the dead are raised to life and the good news is proclaimed to the poor; and blessed is anyone who does not find me a cause of stumbling.' As the men were leaving, Jesus began to talk to the people about John, 'What did you go out into the desert to see? A reed swaying in the breeze? Then what did you go out to see? Someone wearing fine clothes? Look, those who wear fine clothes are to be found in royal palaces. Then what did you go out for? To see a prophet? Yes, I tell you, and more than a prophet. This is the one of whom it is written:

*Look, I am going to send my messenger ahead of you to prepare the way before you.*

'Amen I say to you, of the children born to women, none has been raised up greater than John the Baptist; yet the least in the kingdom of Heaven is greater than he.'

Other readings: Isaiah 35:1–6, 10    Psalm 145 (146)    James 5:7–10

OUR GOSPEL READING, LIKE that of last Sunday, focuses on John the Baptist, but his ministry is now at an end. He is in prison, and martyrdom awaits him. Curiously, he seems to have doubts about Jesus being the Messiah. He who was so confident in proclaiming the one who was to come now seems confused. How can we explain John's uncertainty?

A major feature of the preaching of John the Baptist was the coming of judgement. As we heard in last week's gospel, John expected the Messiah to bring retribution, to separate the chaff from the wheat and to consign the chaff to fire. John must learn that the way of Jesus is different: he brings healing and life, and good news for all.

This gospel reading has a powerful message for us. If it was indeed difficult for John to come to terms with the gospel of mercy, it may well be difficult for us to come to terms with the extraordinary love of God, who offers forgiveness to all. The gospel challenges us to accept in our minds and hearts that the Son of God brings forgiveness, and that the only thing which can deny us salvation and eternal life is our own refusal to be forgiven and loved. The one who is least in the kingdom of heaven knows this, and is 'greater than John'.

*Am I willing to accept the good news of forgiveness for myself and for others?*
*Do I trust the words of Jesus?*
*Let us pray for all those who consider themselves worthless and undeserving of love.*
*Let us pray for those who preach a god of retribution that they may know God's compassion.*

---

# *Fourth Sunday of Advent (Year A)*

## *Matthew 1:18–24*

The birth of Jesus the Messiah happened like this. His mother Mary was betrothed to Joseph; but before they came to live together she was found to be with child through the Holy Spirit. Her husband Joseph, being a righteous man and unwilling to expose her to disgrace, decided to dismiss her quietly. He had this in mind when suddenly an angel of the Lord appeared to him in a dream, saying, 'Joseph, son of David, do not be afraid to take Mary as your wife because the child conceived in her is from the Holy Spirit. She will give birth to a son and you are to name him Jesus, for he will save his people from their sins.' All this took place to fulfil what had been spoken by the Lord through the prophet:

*Look, the virgin is with child and will give birth to a son, and they shall call his name Emmanuel,*

which means 'God-is-with-us'. When Joseph woke from sleep he did what the angel of the Lord had commanded him and took her as his wife.

**Other readings: Isaiah 7:10–14   Psalm 23 (24)   Romans 1:1–7**

WE ARE ACCUSTOMED TO calling the words of the angel Gabriel to Mary 'the Annunciation'. This Sunday's gospel reading perhaps ought to be called 'the annunciation to Joseph'. Joseph is in fact the principal actor in the account of the birth of Jesus in the Gospel of Matthew. Like Mary, he too had to listen for the message of God. Like Mary, he too was invited to play his part in the working out of God's mysterious plan that the Son of God should become man.

This gospel reading, just like the Annunciation to Mary in the Gospel of Luke, gives us the basis for our belief in the virginal conception of Jesus. Here we find an expression of this mystery in the words of the angel to Joseph: 'the child conceived in her is from the Holy Spirit'. The Son of God is born among us in an utterly extraordinary way. The role of Mary as 'virgin mother' is quite unique, and Joseph has to go against his initial inclinations and make the decision to 'take her as his wife'.

In this reading we encounter the first of many verses which Matthew will quote from the Old Testament, declaring that they are 'fulfilled'. The text read at this Mass from the prophet Isaiah speaks of God's constant solidarity with the people. The fulfilment of this same text, which is announced by Matthew in the gospel reading, points to something even greater, the extraordinary intervention of God to bring the Son of God into the world.

*Am I like Joseph willing to go against deeply felt ideas in order to do the will of God?*

*Why would God desire that the Saviour should be born by virginal conception?*

*Let us pray that we may welcome God's new ways as we prepare for Christmas.*

*Let us pray for the people of Palestine and Israel that they may have peace.*

---

# YEAR B

## *First Sunday of Advent (Year B)*

### Mark 13:33-37

Jesus said: 'Take care, stay awake, because you never know when the time will come. It is like a man travelling abroad, leaving his home, and putting his servants in charge, each with his own work to do; and he has told the doorkeeper to stay awake.

'So stay awake, because you do not know when the master of the house is coming, evening, midnight, cockcrow or dawn; when he comes unexpectedly, he must not find you asleep. And what I say to you I say to all: Stay awake!'

**Other readings: Isaiah 63:16-17; 64:1, 3-8   Psalm 79 (80)**
**1 Corinthians 1:3-9**

THE SEASON OF ADVENT begins, and with it we begin to read from the Gospel of Mark. We do not begin at the beginning. The opening verses of the first chapter will be heard next week, and will introduce us to the figure of John the Baptist. Today's reading is from the speech of Jesus about waiting for the return of the Lord. This is the most prominent theme in the first weeks of Advent.

With the coming of the Lord we are forced to wait. This is just as well, for we need to grow in maturity and generosity, in wisdom and love, in order to be ready for our encounter with the one who is wisdom and love made flesh.

Jesus speaks about the future and the end of time in chapter 13 of the Gospel of Mark. This is a gospel with limited accounts of the actual teaching of Jesus. In this chapter Jesus speaks of the trials which people will have to face, and especially of the need for steadfastness among Christians. But the coming of the Lord, to gather together his people from the ends of the earth, is nevertheless assured. The verses we hear today repeatedly encourage us to be watchful for the Lord's coming.

Our reading from the opening verses of St Paul's First Letter to the Corinthians strikes a similar tone. Paul speaks of 'the last day', 'the day of our Lord Jesus Christ'. He assures the Christians of Corinth that they are already united with Jesus and can therefore rely on the fidelity of God.

The reading from the last chapters of the book of Isaiah expresses a deep yearning for the coming of the Lord. 'Oh, that you would tear the heavens open and come down!' The people have experienced exile and the return to their own land is beset with difficulties. Trust in God's goodness is expressed by the image of the potter and his clay: 'we are the clay, you the potter, we are all the work of your hand'.

*Do I wait in joyful hope for the coming of the Lord?*
*What do the words 'stay awake' mean in my life?*
*Let us welcome this liturgical time of waiting which will teach us how to wait for the Lord.*
*Let us welcome the good news again as we begin to read from the Gospel of Mark.*

---

# *Second Sunday of Advent (Year B)*

## *Mark 1:1-8*
The beginning of the gospel about Jesus the Messiah, Son of God.

# SECOND SUNDAY OF ADVENT (YEAR B) 21

As it is written in the prophet Isaiah:

Look, I am sending my messenger in front of you
who will prepare your way.
A voice of one crying in the desert:
Prepare a way for the Lord,
make his paths straight.

John the Baptist was in the desert, proclaiming a baptism of repentance for the forgiveness of sins. All Judaea and all the people of Jerusalem were going out to him, and they were baptised by him in the River Jordan as they confessed their sins. John wore a garment of camel-skin, and a leather belt round his waist, and he ate locusts and wild honey. And as he proclaimed he said, 'After me is coming the one who is more powerful than me, and I am not fit to kneel down and undo the strap of his sandals. I have baptised you with water, but he will baptise you with the Holy Spirit.'

**Other readings: Isaiah 40:1–5, 9–11   Psalm 84 (85)   2 Peter 3:8–14**

OUR GOSPEL READING TODAY is the first eight verses of the Gospel according to Mark. Mark will enter quickly into the adult life and ministry of Jesus. His opening verses deal with the preaching of John the Baptist and culminate in the encounter of Jesus and John at the Jordan. Today's reading includes information about the preaching of John and his words about the coming Messiah.

Mark begins with a profession of faith in Jesus as 'the Christ' ('the Messiah') and the 'Son of God'. These claims for Jesus will be seen to be true as Mark unfolds his story of the life, death and resurrection of Jesus. Mark proclaims 'good news'. What the early preachers and teachers passed on by word of mouth, Mark now puts in writing for the generations to come. It is Mark as the first evangelist who devised this new way of writing, which became known as a 'gospel'.

The coming of Jesus is the fulfillment of the hopes of Israel recorded in the Scriptures. In particular, Mark makes a link between the prophets' words expecting a messenger to prepare for the coming of the Lord and the arrival of John the Baptist. The time of fulfilment has come, the time in which the promises of God will come to pass.

John's call is like that of the prophets. He urges a change of heart among the people. John accompanies his preaching with a ritual washing, a 'baptism of repentance for the forgiveness of sins'. The climax of the reading is John's proclamation that one who is 'more powerful' is coming, one whose sandal-straps John is unworthy to undo. It is he who will baptise with the Holy Spirit.

*Am I ready to hear the good news again?*
*What does the message of John the Baptist mean to me?*
*Let us pray for readiness to change our minds and hearts.*
*Let us pray that like John we will have the right priorities and make the right choices.*

---

## Third Sunday of Advent (Year B)

### John 1:6–8, 19–28

There was a man sent by God.
His name was John.
He came as a witness,
to bear witness to the light,
so that everyone might believe through him.
He was not the light,
he was to bear witness to the light.

This is the witness of John, when the Jews sent to him priests and Levites from Jerusalem to ask him, 'Who are you?' He declared, he did not deny but declared, 'I am not the Messiah.' So they asked, 'What then? Are you Elijah?' He replied, 'I am not.' 'Are you the Prophet?' He answered, 'No.' So they said to him, 'Who are you? So that we may give an answer to those who sent us. What do you say about yourself?' So he said, 'I am, as Isaiah prophesied:

*A voice of one that cries in the desert:*
*prepare a way for the Lord.'*

# THIRD SUNDAY OF ADVENT (YEAR B)

Now they had been sent from the Pharisees, and they put a question to him and said, 'Why then are you baptising if you are not the Messiah nor Elijah nor the Prophet?' John answered them, 'I baptise with water; but among you is standing one whom you do not know, the one who is coming after me; and I am not worthy to undo the strap of his sandal.' This happened at Bethany, on the far side of the Jordan, where John was baptising.

**Other readings: Isaiah 61:1-2, 10-11   Luke 1:46-50, 53-54
1 Thessalonians 5:16-24**

OUR GOSPEL READING FROM the Gospel of John today offers two separate sections from the first chapter of the gospel. What holds them together is that they both deal with John the Baptist, and both sections speak of him as 'a witness'.

The first three verses of this passage are an extract from the great prologue to the gospel, which begins with the words, 'In the beginning was the Word.' In speaking of the entry into the world of the Word of God, the Son sent by the Father, the writer cannot avoid speaking also of John the Baptist, but he makes it quite clear that John was a witness. He was not the Word-Light himself, but only a witness to speak for the light.

The second section of the gospel passage comes immediately after the prologue and gives us details of how John bore his witness to Jesus. It is a characteristic of John that he always points to the one who is greater. He insists that he is simply 'a voice of one that cries in the desert'. He dismisses all the speculation, that he himself might be the Christ, or the prophet to come. His whole ministry is to prepare the way, by baptising with a baptism of repentance, and by proclaiming the coming of the one who truly is the Messiah. To bear witness is the task of every Christian. We bear the name of Christ. Bearing witness to him means bringing his light and truth to those in darkness.

*In what ways should I be imitating the self-effacing humility of the Baptist?*
*What does it mean to be a witness?*
*Let us pray for those called to martyrdom in today's world, that they*

*may have the necessary courage and wisdom.*
*Let us welcome the light, as John did.*

---

# Fourth Sunday of Advent (Year B)

## Luke 1:26-38

In the sixth month the angel Gabriel was sent by God to a town in Galilee called Nazareth, to a virgin betrothed to a man named Joseph, of the House of David; and the virgin's name was Mary. He went in and said to her, 'Rejoice full of grace! The Lord is with you.' She was deeply disturbed by these words and pondered what this greeting could mean, but the angel said to her, 'Do not be afraid, Mary, for you have found favour with God. Look! You will conceive in your womb and bear a son, and you shall name him Jesus. He will be great and will be called Son of the Most High. The Lord God will give him the throne of his ancestor David; he will rule over the House of Jacob for ever and his reign will have no end.' Mary said to the angel, 'But how can this come about, since I have no knowledge of man?' In answer the angel said to her, 'The Holy Spirit will come upon you, and the power of the Most High will overshadow you. And so the child will be holy and will be called Son of God. And see, your cousin Elizabeth also, in her old age, has conceived a son, and she who was said to be barren is now in her sixth month, *for nothing is impossible to God.*' Mary said, 'Here I am, the Lord's servant, let it happen to me as you have said.' And the angel left her.

Other readings: 2 Samuel 7:1-5, 8-12, 14, 16   Psalm 88 (89)
Romans 16:25-27

OUR GOSPEL READING IS the story traditionally called 'the Annunciation'. Luke in fact begins his gospel with two annunciations, the first to Zechariah about the coming birth of his son John the Baptist, and the second to Mary. In both passages the angel announces a birth and speaks of the greatness of the one who is to be born. In the case of Jesus: 'He will be called Son of the Most High.'

What lies at the very heart of this passage is the request of God to Mary and her generous response, by which she allows the Son of God to become a human being within her. Mary hears the word of God and accepts the gift of the child, who is the Word, the Son of God. Paintings of the Annunciation often show Mary at prayer with the book of the Scriptures close by. She has come to know God through prayerful engagement with the Scriptures, and, at this crucial moment in the history of salvation, she responds generously to the call of God in her heart.

Mary was not aware where this would lead her. The words 'Here I am, the Lord's servant' are filled with trust that, whatever lies ahead, God will give her the grace to remain faithful. This willingness to do God's will makes her the first of the disciples of Jesus, and the Mother of the Church.

*How can I be a faithful servant of the Lord, as Mary was?*
*What does this moment of the Incarnation mean to me?*
*Let us pray for trust and perseverance amid the trials which face us.*
*Let us always be grateful for the wonderful deeds of God.*

---

# YEAR C

## *First Sunday of Advent (Year C)*

### Luke 21:25-28, 34-36

Jesus said: 'There will be signs in the sun and moon and stars; on earth distress among nations in confusion at the roaring of the sea and waves, as people faint from fear and expectation of what is coming upon the world, for the powers of the heavens will be shaken. And then they will see the *Son of man coming in a cloud* with power and great glory. When these things begin to take place, stand erect, hold your heads high, because your liberation is drawing near.

'Watch yourselves, so that your hearts are not weighed down by debauchery and drunkenness and the cares of life, and that day comes upon you unexpectedly, like a trap. For it will come upon all those living on the face of the whole earth. Stay awake, praying at all times that you may have the strength to escape all these things that are going to happen, and to take your stand before the Son of man.'

**Other readings: Jeremiah 33:14–16   Psalm 24   1 Thessalonians 3:12–4:2**

IT MAY COME AS a surprise that on the first Sunday of Advent we are suddenly immersed in Luke's version of the long speech of Jesus concerning the future and the end of time. We just need to remember that in Advent we look forward both to the first coming of the Son of God in Bethlehem, and to his glorious return. Our gospel passage speaks of the Son of Man coming 'with power and great glory'. In the Creed we say 'He will come again in glory to judge the living and the dead.' What should our attitude to this coming be? Our gospel reading tells us.

There may be great horrors to witness and endure. We have seen plenty of these in recent years. Jesus tells us not to fear the violence of men, or the devastation nature can bring. Jesus tells us to 'stand erect and hold our heads high'. Jesus speaks of our coming 'liberation'. Since Jesus has conquered sin and death, and demonstrated that the love of God is stronger than both of these, we have no need to fear.

There is also some timely advice for our daily lives that our hearts should not be 'weighed down by debauchery and drunkenness and the cares of life'. Our faith in Jesus means that our very life-style will change and will challenge the values and behaviour of our contemporary society.

Finally, we are told to 'stay awake, praying at all times'. We do not know the day or the hour in which the Lord will call us. But as Christians, though we may still fear the process of death, we know that death is the gateway to eternal life.

*Does my faith really inspire the whole of my life?*
*What is my attitude to the future and the end of my life on earth?*
*Let us pray for all those who are fearful today for whatever reason*
*Let us pray with the early Christians 'Maranatha! Come, Lord Jesus!'*

## *Second Sunday of Advent (Year C)*

### *Luke 3:1-6*

In the fifteenth year of the rule of Tiberius Caesar, when Pontius Pilate was governor of Judaea, Herod tetrarch of Galilee, his brother Philip tetrarch of the territories of Ituraea and Trachonitis, Lysanias tetrarch of Abilene, during the high-priesthood of Annas and Caiaphas, the word of God came to John, the son of Zechariah, in the desert. He went into the whole Jordan area proclaiming a baptism of repentance for the forgiveness of sins, as it is written in the book of the sayings of Isaiah the prophet:

*A voice of one crying in the desert:*
*Prepare a way for the Lord,*
*make his paths straight!*
*Every valley shall be filled in,*
*every mountain and hill be levelled,*
*the crooked shall be straightened*
*and rough places made into smooth roads,*
*and all flesh shall see the salvation of God.*

**Other readings: Baruch 5:1-9    Psalm 125 (126)    Philippians 1:3-6:8-11**

ONE OF THE GREAT characters of the Advent season is John the Baptist, the prophet who prepared the way for Jesus. Later in this gospel Jesus will say: 'Of all the children born of women there is no one greater than John, yet the least in the kingdom of God is greater than he is.'(Luke 7:28) John is truly a great man, but what Jesus will bring will be greater. Our gospel reading this Sunday is from the third chapter of Luke's gospel. Luke has already given an account of John's birth earlier in the gospel. Now Luke introduces the adult John and describes his ministry.

Luke provides an extraordinarily detailed list of the public officials who were in office when John and Jesus began their work. The names of Pontius Pilate and of Herod the tetrarch are easily recognised here. Luke demonstrates that John the Baptist and Jesus enter into the real world of history, a world in which power and position dominate events.

John's work is to travel around the region near the Jordan river, proclaiming 'a baptism of repentance for the forgiveness of sins'. With his baptism John challenges the people to a new start, a change of heart, and to seek the forgiveness of God. If they respond, they will be ready to welcome the Messiah.

At the end of this gospel passage the evangelist gives a lengthy quotation from the book of Isaiah, which Christians consider to have been fulfilled in the coming of the Messiah. We have come to identify the voice in the wilderness with the voice of John. The whole of creation is described as getting ready for the coming of the Lord. Finally, 'all flesh shall see the salvation of God'. Luke makes clear that the Messiah comes to offer salvation to all nations.

*How does the preaching of John the Baptist speak to me today?*
*Do I welcome the coming of Christ as a gift for all the people of the earth?*
*Pray for the wisdom to see that God still cares for the real world of our day.*
*Pray for the zeal of John the Baptist to bear witness to Christ as he did.*

---

# *Third Sunday of Advent (Year C)*

## *Luke 3:10-18*

And the crowds asked John, 'What should we do, then?' He answered them, saying, 'Anyone who has two tunics must share with the one who has none, and anyone who has food must do the same.' Tax collectors, too, came to be baptised, and they said to him, 'Teacher, what should we do?' He said to them, 'Collect no more than the rate appointed for you.' Soldiers also asked him, 'What about us? What should we do?' He said to them, 'No intimidation! No false accusation! Be content with your pay!'

There was a feeling of expectancy among the people; they were all questioning in their hearts whether John might himself be the Messiah. John answered them all by saying, 'I baptise you with water, but one more powerful than me is coming, and I am not fit to undo the strap of

# THIRD SUNDAY OF ADVENT (YEAR C)

his sandals; he will baptise you with the Holy Spirit and with fire. His winnowing-fan is in his hand, to clear his threshing-floor and to gather the wheat into his barn; but the chaff he will burn in a fire that never goes out.' And he proclaimed the good news to the people with many other exhortations too.

**Other readings: Zephaniah 3:14–18  Isaiah 12  Philippians 4:4–7**

Luke's gospel gives prominence to John the Baptist as a social reformer. The question 'What should we do then?' resonates through this reading. The answers are of extraordinary relevance to us. We are called upon to share with the hungry and with the needy, to act with justice and to avoid violence.

Luke also stresses the sense of expectation among the people, who even think that John might be the promised Messiah, the Christ. John then speaks about the mission of the Messiah, describing him as 'more powerful'. John is aware of the battle the Messiah will wage against the forces of evil. The baptism he will bring will demand a choice between working for goodness, truth and justice, or working for lesser and contrary aims.

Notice that Luke tells us that John preaches 'good news'. There is a demanding choice to be made for justice and love, a choice against violence, hatred and selfishness. But the overwhelming atmosphere here is of joyous anticipation of the one who will bring the good news, and who is the good news, the one who will bring healing, forgiveness and new life. During Advent, and particularly on this Third Sunday of Advent, we sense already the profound joy of the coming of the Saviour.

*What demands of justice and non-violence does the gospel bring to me today?*
*Do I welcome the coming of Christ as good news in the deepest sense?*
*Pray for those who strive for a just distribution of the world's riches.*
*Pray for the grace to 'live simply so that others can simply live'.*

## *Fourth Sunday of Advent (Year C)*

## *Luke 1:39–44*

Mary set out at that time and went with haste into the hill country to a town in Judah. She went into Zechariah's house and greeted Elizabeth. Now it happened that when Elizabeth heard Mary's greeting, the child leapt in her womb and Elizabeth was filled with the Holy Spirit. She gave a loud cry and said, 'Blessed are you among women, and blessed is the fruit of your womb. Why has this happened to me, that the mother of my Lord should come to me? Look, as soon as your greeting reached my ears, the child in my womb leapt for joy.

**Other readings: Micah 5:1–4    Psalm 79 (80)    Hebrews 10:5–10**

ON THE DAYS BEFORE the feast of Christmas, and on this final Sunday, the gospel read at Mass is taken from the first chapter of Matthew's gospel or the first chapter of Luke's. These two gospel-writers give us accounts of the birth of Jesus, and in Luke's case the birth of John the Baptist too. Luke describes Mary as the 'kinswoman' of Elizabeth (Luke 1:36), and stresses how deeply related the mission of John the Baptist is to the mission of Christ.

Today's gospel passage is unique because it presents a meeting between the mothers of the two men, each carrying in their wombs the children soon to be born. The story, known as the 'Visitation', follows the account of the Annunciation to Mary of the coming birth of the Saviour, which ended with Mary's 'Yes' to God and her words, 'let it happen to me as you have said'. (Luke 1:38)

Commentators on this gospel story have often stressed the kindness of Mary in going to the assistance of Elizabeth in her time of need. The story also has a deeper significance, for it is the first meeting between the Messiah and the one who will prepare the way for him. The first words of Elizabeth to Mary are familiar as part of the 'Hail, Mary': 'Blessed art thou among women, and blessed is the fruit of thy womb!' Luke tells us that the child in the womb of Elizabeth recognised the coming of the Lord, the Messiah. What John will do during his adult life, preparing the people for the coming of the Messiah, is anticipated here in the tender meeting of

# FOURTH SUNDAY OF ADVENT (YEAR C)

two pregnant mothers. As Mary welcomed the coming of the Lord into her body, now John, as yet unborn, welcomes his arrival too.

If we continue to read the gospel beyond today's passage we hear the words of Mary's hymn of thanksgiving, the *Magnificat*, prayed daily by the Church at Evening Prayer.

*What can we learn from the behaviour and attitude of Mary and Elizabeth?*
*How will the coming of Christ change me?*
*Pray for all mothers that they may welcome the children of their womb.*
*Pray for a deep spirit of thanksgiving for God's goodness.*

# CHRISTMAS

## *The Nativity of Our Lord (Christmas Day)*

### *John 1:1-18*
In the beginning was the Word:
the Word was with God
and the Word was God.
He was with God in the beginning.
Through him all things came into being,
not one thing came into being except through him.
What has come into being in him was life,
life that was the light of all people;
and light shines in darkness,
and darkness could not overpower it.

There was a man sent by God.
His name was John.
He came as a witness,
to bear witness to the light,
so that everyone might believe through him.
He was not the light,
he was to bear witness to the light.

The true light
that gives light to everyone
was coming into the world.
He was in the world
and the world came into being through him,
and the world did not know him.
He came to what was his own
and his own people did not accept him.
But to those who did accept him
he gave power to become children of God,
to those who believed in his name,
who were born not from blood,

or from the will of the flesh,
or from human will
but from God himself.
The Word became flesh,
and lived among us,
and we saw his glory,
the glory as of an only-begotten Son of the Father,
full of grace and truth.

John witnesses to him and cried out, saying,
'This is the one of whom I said:
He who comes after me
has passed ahead of me
because he was before me.'

Indeed, from his fullness
we have all received,
grace upon grace,
for the Law was given through Moses,
grace and truth came through Jesus Christ.
No one has ever seen God;
it is the only-begotten Son,
who is close to the Father's heart,
who has made him known.

**Other readings: Isaiah 52:7–10   Psalm 97 (98)   Hebrews 1:1–6**

THREE SEPARATE SETS OF readings are provided for the three Masses of Christmas Day: the Mass during the Night, the Mass at Dawn and the Mass during the Day. The readings considered here are those of the Mass during the day.

The opening words of the Gospel according to John, known as the Prologue, offer a rich reflection on the mystery of the human birth of the Son of God. The evangelist refers to him as 'the Word', for God has finally spoken his fullest word to the human race. As the reading from the Letter to the Hebrews states, God having spoken at many times in the past 'in the last days has spoken to us through his Son'. The Prologue also refers to Jesus as 'the Light', for he brings truth and direction in our darkness. The darkness of sin and death cannot overcome the light of Christ. The evangelist speaks of the rejection of the Word by many, but also of the power given to those who do accept him, to all those who believe in him. The feast of Christ's birth invites us to renew that faith and welcome the Word of light into our lives again.

*Do I appreciate that the birth of Christ is God's loving
   invitation to change my life?*
*Do I welcome the Word of life and light into the dark corners
   of my life?*
*We pray that the feast of Christmas will bring many to
   reconsider the Christian message.*
*Let us open our hearts to the grace and truth of God.*

---

# *Feast of the Holy Family (Year A)*

## *Matthew 2:13-15, 19-23*

After they had left, see, an angel of the Lord appeared to Joseph in a dream and said, 'Get up. Take the child and his mother, flee into Egypt and stay there until I tell you, for Herod intends to search for the child to destroy him.' So Joseph got up and, taking the child and his mother by night, left for Egypt and stayed there until the death of Herod. This was to fulfil what had been spoken by the Lord through the prophet, saying:

*I called my son out of Egypt.*

When Herod had died, see, an angel of the Lord appeared in a dream to Joseph in Egypt saying, 'Get up. Take the child and his mother and go to the land of Israel, for those who were seeking the child's life are dead.' So Joseph got up and, taking the child and his mother, went to the land of Israel. But when he learnt that Archelaus was king of Judaea in place of his father, Herod, he was afraid to go there, and, being warned in a dream, he withdrew to the region of Galilee. There he settled in a town called

Nazareth so that what had been spoken through the prophets should be fulfilled:

'He will be called a Nazarene'.

**Other readings: Ecclesiasticus 3:2–6,12–14　　Psalm 127 (128)
Colossians 3:12–21**

AS IN THE GOSPEL reading for the Fourth Sunday of Advent, Joseph is once again the main character in today's gospel reading. Soon after his birth the life of Jesus is put at risk. Like Joseph in the Book of Genesis, who is the saviour of his people in Egypt, this Joseph too is the saviour of his family from the power of Herod, king of the Jews.

Joseph is portrayed as always ready to listen to the angel of the Lord. He listens as God speaks in his heart. Having been willing to take the pregnant Mary into his home, he now takes her and the child she has borne on a difficult journey to a foreign land. The return to the land of Israel is equally traumatic, since Joseph settles as a newcomer in the region of Galilee. Joseph demonstrates steadfastness in his commitment to protecting his family, but also willingness to respond when what is asked of him is new and unexpected.

The gospel makes clear from its opening pages that Jesus' entry into this world brings with it a vulnerability which will be seen most clearly at the cross. The life of the child Jesus is put at risk due to the lust for power of the leaders of his day. Herod the king in fact never hesitated to use violent means to protect his kingship from threats both real and imagined.

*How does this gospel reading help us understand the deeper
　　meaning of Christmas?*
*Does the courage of Joseph show us how to react to violence in
　　our own time?*
*We pray for all fathers and mothers that they may always do
　　what is best for their children.*
*We pray for all children who are neglected and ill-treated.*

## *Feast of the Holy Family (Year B)*

### *Luke 2:22–40*
And when the days were complete for them to be purified in keeping with the Law of Moses, they took him up to Jerusalem to present him to the Lord – as it is written in the Law of the Lord: *Every first-born male shall be called holy to the Lord* – and also to offer in sacrifice, in accordance with what is prescribed in the Law of the Lord, *a pair of turtledoves or two young pigeons.* Now in Jerusalem there was a man named Simeon. He was a righteous and devout man, looking forward to the consolation of Israel, and the Holy Spirit rested on him. It had been revealed to him by the Holy Spirit that he would not see death until he had seen the Christ of the Lord. Prompted by the Spirit he came into the Temple; and when the parents brought in the child Jesus to do for him what the Law required, Simeon himself took him into his arms and blessed God and said:

Now, Master, you are letting your servant
go in peace according to your word;
for my eyes have seen your salvation
which you have made ready in the presence of all nations;
a light for revelation to the gentiles
and for the glory of your people Israel.

As the child's father and mother were wondering at the things that were being said about him, Simeon blessed them and said to Mary his mother, 'Look, he is destined for the fall and for the rise of many in Israel, destined to be a sign that is opposed – and a sword will pierce your soul too – so that the thoughts of many may be laid bare.'

There was a prophetess, too, Anna the daughter of Phanuel, of the tribe of Asher. She was advanced in years, having lived with her husband seven years after her marriage, then as a widow to the age of eighty-four. She never left the Temple, worshipping night and day with fasting and prayer. She came up just at that moment and began to praise God;

and to speak about the child to all who looked forward to the deliverance of Jerusalem.

When they had completed everything according to the Law of the Lord, they went back to Galilee, to their own town of Nazareth. And the child grew and became strong, filled with wisdom, and God's favour was on him.

**Other readings: Ecclesiasticus 3:2–6, 12–14    Psalm 127 (128)
Colossians 3:12–21**

THE PRESENTATION IN THE Temple has a profound significance. Jesus, the Son of God, obeys the Law of God as he is presented in the Temple by Mary and Joseph. His parents are faithful Jews, who abide by the religious laws of the time. This first entry of the Son of God into the house of God speaks of his willingness to do the will of the Father.

The old man Simeon is inspired by the Holy Spirit to speak about the child, and about his mother. Simeon points to Jesus as the fulfilment of the hopes and longings of his own people, and of all peoples. He is to be the 'glory of Israel', but also a 'light for the gentiles'. Simeon tells Mary that the child is to be 'a sign that is opposed'. We can accept or reject him. Mary, who said her generous 'Yes' to God, will be drawn into the suffering of her Son.

*What does this gospel tell us about the coming of Jesus?*
*What does this gospel tell us about the role of parents?*
*Let us pray for all parents, that they will lead their children in*
    *goodness and truth.*
*Let us ask for understanding of the place of suffering in Christian life.*

---

# *Feast of the Holy Family (Year C)*

## *Luke 2:41–52*

Every year his parents used to go to Jerusalem for the festival of the Passover. When he was twelve years old, they went up for the festival as usual. When the days of the festival were over and they set off home, the boy Jesus stayed behind in

# FEAST OF THE HOLY FAMILY (YEAR C)

Jerusalem without his parents knowing it. They assumed he was in the party, and after a day's journey they started looking for him among their relations and acquaintances. When they could not find him they went back to Jerusalem looking for him.

It happened that, after three days, they found him in the Temple, sitting among the teachers, listening to them, and asking them questions; and all those who heard him were astounded at his intelligence and his replies. When they saw him they were overcome, and his mother said to him, 'Child, why have you treated us like this? See, your father and I have been searching for you anxiously.' He replied, 'Why were you looking for me? Did you not know that I must be in my Father's house?' But they did not understand what he was saying to them.

He went down with them then and came to Nazareth and lived under their authority. His mother stored up all these things in her heart. And Jesus increased in wisdom, in stature, and in divine and human favour.

**Other readings: Ecclesiasticus 3:2–6, 12–14   Psalm 127 (128)
Colossians 3:12–21**

TODAY'S GOSPEL GIVES US a rare glimpse of the 'hidden life' of Jesus, the years he spent under the care of Mary and Joseph. Luke displays their fidelity to their Jewish faith, and he underlines the autonomy of the young Jesus in staying behind in Jerusalem. We encounter the mystery of the Son of God who has become man. He is fully human and subject to his parents, but from his earliest years Jesus is involved in his Father's affairs. The Temple doctors are astounded at the learning of Jesus, and this prepares for the astonishment of the crowds once his public ministry begins.

The story reaches its climax with the finding of Jesus by his parents. Luke stresses the anxiety of Mary, foreshadowing the three days of anguish when Jesus dies. His parents did not understand Jesus' words, but Mary will 'store these things in her heart'. She is the contemplative who receives the word and puts it into practice. Luke brings the stories of Jesus' early life to an end by reminding us that Jesus grew in wisdom as the years passed.

*What does this story of Jesus' adolescence really teach us?*
*How is Luke preparing us for later events in the gospel story?*
*Let us pray for patience with ourselves and with others as we seek to grow in wisdom.*
*Let us pray for all our young people that they will be open to doing God's will.*

---

# The Solemnity of Mary, Mother of God

## Luke 2:16–21

So they went in haste and found Mary and Joseph, and the baby lying in the manger. When they saw this, they made known what they had been told about this child, and everyone who heard it was astonished at what the shepherds said to them. But Mary treasured all these things and pondered them in her heart. And the shepherds went back glorifying and praising God for all they had heard and seen, just as they had been told.

When the eight days were complete to circumcise the child, he was called Jesus, the name the angel had given him before he was conceived in the womb.

**Other readings: Numbers 6:22–27   Psalm 66 (67)   Galatians 4:4–7**

MOST OF THIS GOSPEL reading for the feast of Mary, Mother of God, the octave day of Christmas and the first day of the calendar year, has already been heard as the gospel for the Dawn Mass of Christmas Day. The final verse is added today. It is particularly appropriate, since this is the eighth day, the octave day, of Christmas.

But there is a more important reason why reading these verses today, one week after Christmas Day, is different. We are asked to focus on the role and on the behaviour of Mary, the mother of the Messiah. This feast on the octave day of Christmas was instituted in the liturgical reforms of the Second Vatican Council. It replaces the feast of the Circumcision of our Lord. It is most appropriate that we should focus on Mary on this day.

The coming into a human life of the Son of God could only

happen with the collaboration of this humble woman of Nazareth. God respects our human freedom. Mary was invited to work for God in this unique way. Her response to the invitation was a courageous and generous 'yes'. Her *fiat* is a turning point in history for it enables the Son of God to become a human being. Her *fiat* is an example to all those who, like Mary, endeavour to do the will of God by following Jesus.

On this solemn feast we continue to commemorate the birth of Jesus. We acknowledge the consequences of this birth for us, as St Paul writes in the reading from the Letter to the Galatians: 'at the appointed time God sent his Son, born of a woman' in order to redeem us and offer us adoption as children of God. Our first reading, from the Book of Numbers, invokes God's blessing on God's people as the new year begins.

*Do I appreciate the courage and love of Mary and see her as an example?*

*Do I imitate Mary's silence and her pondering of God's goodness in her heart?*

*We pray that we may follow the example of Mary, the first servant of Jesus Christ, who listened for God's word and responded with generosity.*

*We open our hearts to God at the beginning of a new year, that God may bless us and keep us day by day.*

---

# *Second Sunday after Christmas*

## *John 1:1-18*

In the beginning was the Word:
the Word was with God
and the Word was God.
He was with God in the beginning.
Through him all things came into being,
not one thing came into being except through him.
What has come into being in him was life,
life that was the light of all people;
and light shines in darkness,
and darkness could not overpower it.

There was a man sent by God.
His name was John.
He came as a witness,
to bear witness to the light,
so that everyone might believe through him.
He was not the light,
he was to bear witness to the light.

The true light
that gives light to everyone
was coming into the world.
He was in the world
and the world came into being through him,
and the world did not know him.
He came to what was his own
and his own people did not accept him.
But to those who did accept him
he gave power to become children of God,
to those who believed in his name,
who were born not from blood,
or from the will of the flesh,
or from human will
but from God himself.
The Word became flesh,
and lived among us,
and we saw his glory,
the glory as of an only-begotten Son of the Father,
full of grace and truth.

John witnesses to him and cried out, saying,
'This is the one of whom I said:
He who comes after me
has passed ahead of me
because he was before me.'

Indeed, from his fullness
we have all received,
grace upon grace,
for the Law was given through Moses,

# SECOND SUNDAY AFTER CHRISTMAS

grace and truth came through Jesus Christ.
No one has ever seen God;
it is the only-begotten Son,
who is close to the Father's heart,
who has made him known.

**Other readings: Ecclesiasticus 24:1-2, 8-12   Psalm 147 (148)
Ephesians 1:3-6, 15-18**

THIS SUNDAY OF THE Christmas season offers the opportunity to reflect quietly with the help of the Scripture readings on the deeper meaning of the coming of Christ. Our first reading, from the extensive writings of the sage known as Ben Sira, offers a reflection on how 'Wisdom' pitches her tent among the people of God. The one who was from the beginning 'takes root in a privileged people'. These words are fulfilled in the becoming flesh of the Son of God. This is momentously expressed in the first chapter of the Fourth Gospel, read today: 'the Word became flesh and lived among us'. He 'pitched his tent among us'.

John the evangelist calls Jesus 'the Word', for in him God has spoken his fullest word to the human race. The Prologue also refers to Jesus as 'the true Light', for he brings truth and direction in our darkness. The darkness of sin and death cannot overcome the light of Christ. Many will reject the Word, but those who accept him become children of God. Our gospel also refers to the witness of John the Baptist, who points to one greater than himself.

We have all received from the fulness of the Word. In the opening of the Letter to the Ephesians we bless God who has chosen us in Christ to be adopted sons and daughters.

*How can we ever fathom the marvelous love of God who humbles himself to share in our humanity?*
*Do I appreciate or simply forget that I am an adopted child of God?*
*We pray that the feast of Christmas will shed light on our darkness.*
*Let us open our hearts to the grace and truth which come to us in Christ.*

## *Solemnity of the Epiphany*

### *Matthew 2:1–12*

After Jesus had been born at Bethlehem in Judaea during the time of King Herod, suddenly some wise men from the east came to Jerusalem, asking, 'Where is the child born king of the Jews? For we saw his star at its rising and have come to worship him.' When King Herod heard this he was perturbed, and the whole of Jerusalem with him. He called together all the chief priests and the scribes of the people, and enquired of them where the Messiah was to be born. They told him, 'At Bethlehem in Judaea, for this is what was written by the prophet:

*And you, Bethlehem,*
*in the land of Judah,*
*you are by no means the least*
*among the leaders of Judah,*
*for from you will come a leader*
*who will shepherd my people Israel.'*

Then Herod secretly summoned the wise men and made certain from them the exact time when the star had appeared, and sent them on to Bethlehem, saying, 'Go and find out accurately about the child, and when you have found him, report back to me, so that I too may go to worship him.' When they had heard the king, they set out. And see, the star they had seen at its rising went before them until it halted over the place where the child was. Seeing the star, they rejoiced with very great joy, and going into the house they saw the child with Mary, his mother, and falling down they worshipped him. Then, opening their treasure chests, they offered him gifts of gold and frankincense and myrrh. But having been warned in a dream not to go back to Herod, they returned to their own country by a different way.

Other readings: Isaiah 60:1–6   Psalm 71 (72)   Ephesians 3:2–3, 5–6

THE STORY OF THE Magi carries with it an extraordinary richness. In it the evangelist teaches us about the mission of the Son of God. Jesus is 'made manifest' (epiphany = manifestation) as Messiah not only for his own people, but for those who come 'from the east', for all the peoples of the earth. At the same time this is the Messiah heralded by the prophets. The Scriptures are fulfilled.

This Messiah is born into danger, as the cruel tyrant, known to history as 'Herod the Great', is the first to threaten his life. The gift of myrrh alludes to the death he is to suffer. The presentation of gifts from the peoples of the world completes the Christmas scene. The Magi represent the nations, but also the age-old quest among the peoples of the earth for true wisdom. This wisdom is found in Christ.

*What lies at the heart of the epiphany story?*
*How is Matthew preparing us for later events in the gospel story?*
*Let us rejoice with the peoples of the whole world that God's love has been revealed in the birth of Jesus.*
*We pray for a growing solidarity with those all over the world who suffer.*

---

# *The Baptism of the Lord (Year A)*

## *Matthew 3:13–17*

Then Jesus came from Galilee to the Jordan to be baptised by John. John tried to prevent him, saying, 'I need to be baptised by you, and yet do you come to me?' But Jesus replied, 'Leave it for the time being; for so it is fitting that we should fulfil all righteousness.' Then he allowed him. And when Jesus had been baptised he at once came up from the water, and see, the heavens opened and he saw the Spirit of God descending like a dove and coming down on him. And see, a voice from heaven, 'This is my Son, the Beloved, in whom I am well pleased.'

Other readings: Isaiah 42:1–4, 6–7  Psalm 28 (29)  Acts 10:34–38

## THE BAPTISM OF THE LORD (YEAR A)

THE FEAST OF THE Baptism of the Lord brings the Christmas season to an end. The Solemnity of the Epiphany led us to reflect on the mission of the Lord to bring salvation to all nations. Now we see that mission begin with the reporting by the evangelists of a most significant action of the adult Jesus.

John the Baptist, who has been baptising and preaching repentance as well as instilling hope in the people to look forward to the 'one who is to come', now comes face to face with the Messiah. Jesus, although he is without sin, nevertheless wishes to undergo with the people the baptism of repentance. It is not surprising that John is perplexed and initially unwilling to comply.

The words of Jesus that they should 'fulfil all righteousness' suggest that we are dealing here with the fidelity of the Son of God to enter fully into our damaged humanity.

As in the other synoptic gospels (Mark and Luke) the baptism of Jesus by John is accompanied by a vision and a voice. Jesus sees the Spirit descend on him. It is the Spirit mentioned by Peter to Cornelius in our second reading when he says that 'God anointed him with the Holy Spirit and power'.

The words addressed to Jesus, 'This is my Son, the Beloved; in whom I am well pleased', echo the words of God in the first reading from the book of Isaiah. This passage is known as the first 'Servant Song'. The prophet presents to us the qualities of true servanthood, qualities which are amply lived out in the life and mission of Jesus. The baptism of Jesus is a clear expression of his will to stand alongside sinners in order to bring us the fulness of life.

*How has the celebration of the Christmas season inspired your faith and work?*
*Why did Jesus seek baptism from John?*
*We thank God for the incarnation, that the Son of God has taken on himself the joys and sorrows of the human condition.*
*We pray for fidelity and maturity in living out our own Christian calling to be servants.*

# The Baptism of the Lord (Year B)

## Mark 1:7–11

And as he proclaimed he said, 'After me is coming the one who is more powerful than me, and I am not fit to kneel down and undo the strap of his sandals. I have baptised you with water, but he will baptise you with the Holy Spirit.'

It was in those days that Jesus came from Nazareth in Galilee and was baptised in the Jordan by John. And at once, as he was coming up out of the water, he saw the heavens torn apart and the Spirit, like a dove, descending on him. And a voice came from heaven, 'You are my Son, the Beloved; in you I am well pleased.'

Other readings: Isaiah 42:1–4, 6–7   Psalm 28 (29)   Acts 10:34–38

THE CHRISTMAS SEASON CONCLUDES with the Feast of the Baptism of the Lord. It is appropriate that this is so, for Jesus comes into the world not to live in obscurity but to perform the mission given him by the Father with the power of the Holy Spirit. His baptism comes at the start of his public life and heralds his ministry.

The account of the work of John the Baptist in the Gospel of Mark is quite brief. He preaches 'a baptism of repentance for the forgiveness of sins'. John urges people to change their hearts and lives in preparation for the Messiah. The Gospels of Matthew and Luke give far fuller accounts of the preaching of the Baptist, and add significantly to the brief account in the Gospel of Mark.

In the passage for this feast John proclaims that the one who is to come will be 'more powerful than me'. John's preaching attracted crowds of people and had a strong effect on them. When Jesus comes, John implies, he will confront evil in all its forms with the power of the Spirit. This 'more powerful' one will bring a baptism which will have a deeper and more lasting effect, for it will be baptism in the Holy Spirit.

The evangelist does not dwell long on the actual baptism of Jesus, this clear demonstration of his solidarity with all those who need healing and forgiveness. Mark puts the emphasis on the vision Jesus sees and the voice he hears. The baptism story shows Jesus to be the Spirit-filled Servant of God. His mission reflects that of the servant described in those passages in the second part of the Book of Isaiah known as the 'servant songs', one of which is our first reading. Jesus is the beloved Son of God, who will always do what pleases the Father.

*How appropriate is it to conclude the Christmas celebration with the feast of the Baptism of Jesus?*

*What was the purpose of Jesus' baptism by John?*

*We pray for a deeper sense of awe at God's love for all creation, which is displayed at Christmas.*

*We pray that in the coming year we may grow in strength as servants of the Lord.*

---

# *The Baptism of the Lord (Year C)*

## *Luke 3:15-16, 21-22*

There was a feeling of expectancy among the people; they were all questioning in their hearts whether John might himself be the Messiah. John answered them all by saying, 'I baptise you with water, but one more powerful than me is coming, and I am not fit to undo the strap of his sandals; he will baptise you with the Holy Spirit and with fire.'

Now it happened that while all the people were being baptised and while Jesus, after his own baptism, was at prayer, heaven opened and the Holy Spirit descended on him in a physical form, like a dove. And a voice came from heaven, 'You are my Son, the Beloved; in you I am well pleased.'

**Other readings: Isaiah 42:1-4, 6-7  Psalm 28 (29)  Acts 10:34-38**

THE FINAL FEAST OF THE Christmas season is the Feast of the Baptism of the Lord. Having celebrated his birth and his manifestation as the Messiah for all nations, it is appropriate to conclude the season with the event which begins his public ministry.

Our gospel reading contains two verses about the work of John the Baptist. John was a major figure during Advent, for it was he who prepared the way for the coming of Christ. Now we see him as

# THE BAPTISM OF THE LORD (YEAR C)

the one who offered baptism to Christ in the Jordan. John clarifies that he himself is not the Christ. He knew he was a servant, one who would point the way to someone 'more powerful'. John was a strong and effective preacher of forgiveness and new life. Jesus will show his power above all by his might works of healing. John alludes to the Spirit who will accompany the work of Jesus and to his new kind of baptism.

The evangelist Luke presents the baptism of Jesus in a unique way. Jesus, who is in no need of conversion himself, shows solidarity with all those coming to John for baptism. Luke hardly mentions the baptism itself but concentrates on the manifestation of the Spirit and on the voice heard. As so often in the Gospel of Luke, Jesus is presented as praying after his baptism. It is as if he is at prayer as he awaits the coming of the Holy Spirit.

Most remarkable is Luke's description of the Spirit 'in bodily form', whereby the evangelist insists on the reality of the Spirit's presence. The vision is seen by all, and the voice similarly to be heard by all. The words are inspired by the Servant Song which is our first reading from the Book of Isaiah: 'Here is my servant, in whom my soul delights.'

*Why did Jesus seek baptism from John?*
*How similar is John's baptism to that of Jesus?*
*Let us seek a renewal of the grace of our own baptism.*
*Let us prepare to accompany Jesus in Luke's story of his ministry throughout the coming weeks.*

# Lent

# YEAR A

## *First Sunday of Lent (Year A)*

### *Matthew 4:1–11*

Then Jesus was led by the Spirit out into the desert to be put to the test by the devil. He fasted for forty days and forty nights, after which he was hungry, and the tempter came and said to him, 'If you are Son of God, tell these stones to turn into loaves.' But he replied, 'It is written:

*A human lives not on bread alone*
*but on every word that comes from the mouth of God.'*

Then the devil took him to the holy city and set him on the parapet of the Temple, and said to him, 'If you are Son of God throw yourself down, for it is written:

*He will give his angels orders about you,*
*and they will carry you in their hands*
*in case you trip on a stone.'*

Jesus said to him, 'It is also written:

*Do not put the Lord your God to the test.'*

Next, taking him to a very high mountain, the devil showed him all the kingdoms of the world and their glory. And he said to him, 'These shall all be yours if you fall at my feet and worship me.' Then Jesus replied, 'Away with you, Satan! For it is written:

*The Lord your God shall you worship*
*and him alone shall you serve.'*

## FIRST SUNDAY OF LENT (YEAR A)

Then the devil left him, and see, angels appeared and looked after him.

**Other readings: Genesis 2: 7–9, 3:1–7   Psalm 50 (51)   Romans 5:12–19**

THE READINGS SET BEFORE us for the Sundays of Lent are extraordinarily rich. On the first Sunday the gospel is always that of the temptations of Jesus, read from one of the synoptic gospels (Matthew, Mark and Luke). This year it is Matthew's account which is read.

Jesus, filled with the Spirit received at his baptism, is now led by the same Spirit to the place of encounter with the devil. He who was willing to undergo the baptism usually reserved for sinners now submits to the challenge of evil. He who showed solidarity with sinners now confronts the power of sin.

There is a profound mystery here. The sinless one, who comes to save sinners, is nevertheless tempted, for Jesus in his humanity has the same power of choice that we have. While we frequently succumb to the lure of evil, Jesus never does. Three distinct temptations invite him to abuse his miraculous powers for selfish ends (turning stones into bread), to manipulate his relationship with the Father (leaping from the temple parapet), and to collude with evil to gain dominion over the world (worshipping the devil).

Jesus confounds the devil on each occasion by quoting from the Book of Deuteronomy. The Scriptures urge us to pursue what is good and to worship the one, true God. The behaviour of Jesus in the gospel contrasts sharply with that of Adam and Eve in the reading from Genesis as they succumb to temptation. St Paul, writing to the Romans in the second reading, explains the effects of the disobedience of Adam and the obedience of Jesus.

*From where does Jesus derive his strength in his battle with evil?*
*To what extent do the Scriptures inspire my decisions?*
*Pray for the courage to unmask the deceptive power of evil.*
*Pray for the wisdom to reject selfishness and the strength to confront evil.*

# Second Sunday of Lent (Year A)

## Matthew 17:1-9

Six days later, Jesus took with him Peter and James and his brother John and led them up a high mountain on their own. In their presence he was transfigured: his face shone like the sun and his clothes became as dazzling as light. And suddenly Moses and Elijah appeared to them, talking with him. Then Peter spoke to Jesus, saying, 'Lord, it is wonderful for us to be here; if you want me to, I will make three shelters here, one for you, one for Moses and one for Elijah.' He was still speaking when suddenly a bright cloud covered them with shadow, and suddenly from the cloud there came a voice which said, 'This is my Son, the Beloved; he enjoys my favour. Listen to him.' When they heard this, the disciples fell on their faces, overcome with fear. But Jesus came up and touched them, saying, 'Stand up, do not be afraid.' And when they raised their eyes they saw no one but Jesus himself alone.

As they came down from the mountain Jesus gave them this order, 'Tell no one about this vision until the Son of man has risen from the dead.'

**Other readings:** Genesis 12:1–4   Psalm 32 (33)   2 Timothy 1:8–10

ON THE SECOND SUNDAY of Lent the gospel of the Transfiguration is always read, from one or other of the three synoptic gospels (Matthew, Mark and Luke). This year it is Matthew's account which is read. What is it that makes this story appropriate at this time?

The story recounts an experience of Jesus that three disciples shared, but which they are told must remain secret until after he has risen from the dead. The experience astonishes the disciples, for they see Jesus transformed, transfigured, as they have never seen him before.

To understand the meaning of this event we should remember that in the gospel story Jesus has just told the disciples that he foresees his own Passion and death. They react with horror. The Transfiguration serves to put their fear in a broader context. Going to his death, Jesus nevertheless trusts that the Father will raise him from the dead. The experience of the Transfiguration, the details of which are quite difficult to grasp, gives these three chosen disciples a glimpse of something beyond suffering and death.

The reading from the book of Genesis may seem to have little connection, but here too we are aware of a journey, the journey of Abraham into the unknown as he trusts God to be with him. The journey of Jesus to the cross is similar. If we have trust in God we too can 'bear the hardships for the sake of the Good News', as the second reading asks.

*How might the story of the Transfiguration give us hope?*
*Have I ever experienced anything like transfiguration in my own life?*
*We pray that we may persevere in trust, like Jesus and Abraham.*
*We pray for a broader vision, that we may be more aware of the things*
  *of God, and of God's goodness.*

---

# *Third Sunday of Lent (Year A)*

## *John 4:5–42*

So he came to the Samaritan town called Sychar, near the land that Jacob had given to his son Joseph. Jacob's well was there and Jesus, tired by the journey, was sitting by the well. It was about noon, when a Samaritan woman came to draw water. Jesus said to her, 'Give me a drink.' His disciples had gone into the town to buy food. The Samaritan said to him, 'How is it that you, a Jew, ask me, a Samaritan woman, for a drink?' – for Jews do not associate with Samaritans. Jesus replied to her:

'If you knew what God is offering
and who it is saying to you, "Give me a drink",
 you would have asked him,
and he would have given you living water.'

She answered, 'Sir, you have no bucket, and the well is deep. Where do you get this living water? Are you a greater man than our father Jacob, who gave us this well and drank from it, himself and his sons and his cattle?' Jesus replied:

'Whoever drinks of this water
will be thirsty again;
but anyone who drinks of the water that I shall
    give
will never be thirsty again:
the water that I shall give
will become an inner spring of water, welling up to eternal life.'

The woman said to him, 'Sir, give me this water, so that I may never be thirsty or go on coming here to draw water.' Jesus said to her, 'Go and call your husband and come back here.' The woman answered him saying, 'I have no husband.' Jesus said to her, 'You are right to say, "I have no husband"; for you have had five men, and the one you now have is not your husband. You spoke the truth there.' The woman said to him, 'Sir, I see you are a prophet. Our fathers worshipped on this mountain, though you say that the place where people should worship is in Jerusalem.' Jesus said:

'Believe me, woman, the hour is coming
when you will worship the Father
neither on this mountain nor in Jerusalem.
You worship what you do not know;
we worship what we do know;
for salvation is from the Jews.
But the hour is coming – and is now here –
when true worshippers will worship the Father in spirit and
    truth,
for such are the worshippers
whom the Father seeks.
God is spirit,
and those who worship him
must worship in spirit and truth.'

The woman said to him, 'I know that Messiah, the one called Christ, is coming; and when he comes he will declare everything.' Jesus said, 'I am he, the one who is speaking to you.'

At this point his disciples returned and were surprised to find him speaking to a woman, but none of them asked,

'What do you want?' or, 'Why are you talking to her?'

The woman left her water jar and went off to the town and said to the people, 'Come and see a man who has told me everything I have ever done. Could this be the Messiah?' They came out of the town and they made their way towards him.

Meanwhile, the disciples were urging him, 'Rabbi, have something to eat'; but he said, 'I have food to eat that you do not know about.' So the disciples said to one another, 'Has someone brought him food?' But Jesus said:

'My food is to do the will of the one who sent me,
and to complete his work.
Do you not say,
"Four months and then the harvest"?
Well, I tell you,
look around you, look at the fields;
they are white for the harvest!
Already the reaper is being paid his wages,
already he is bringing in the grain for eternal life,
so that sower and reaper may rejoice together.
For here the proverb holds true:
one sows, another reaps;
I sent you to reap
a harvest for which you did not labour.
Others have laboured;
and you have come into the rewards of their labour.'

Many Samaritans of that town believed in him on the strength of the words of the woman's witness, 'He told me everything I have done.' So, when the Samaritans came to him, they asked him to stay with them. He stayed there for two days, and many more came to believe on the strength of the words he spoke to them; and they said to the woman, 'We believe no longer because of what you told us; we have heard for ourselves and we know that this is truly the Saviour of the world.'

**Other readings: Exodus 17:3–7   Psalm 94 (95)   Romans 5:1–2, 5–8**

FOR THIS AND THE following two Sundays we shall be hearing lengthy passages from the Gospel of John, chosen to help us prepare for Easter and the celebration of our new life in Jesus Christ.

The Samaritan woman gradually learns more about Jesus and what he offers her. Her journey reflects our own journey of faith. The dialogue begins with Jesus seeking a drink and then offering 'living water' to the woman. Water gives life. The 'living water' given by Jesus points to eternal life. As the dialogue continues it is established that Jesus is not only a prophet, but the Messiah. The woman's eyes are gradually opening, enough for her to go and tell her townspeople. At the end they too come to believe, not simply due to her testimony but because they have themselves heard the preaching of Jesus.

In the middle of the chapter we hear about the need to worship 'in spirit and truth' (verse 23). Jesus comes, and this chapter shows it, to bring together the Jews, the Samaritans and all the nations of the earth in the worship of the one, true God.

*How is the Samaritan woman a model for our faith journey?*
*Are we also sometimes slow to understand the gifts of God?*
*We pray that we may worship the Lord in spirit and truth.*
*We pray for the courage to lead others to Christ, the teacher who gives us 'living water'.*

---

## *Fourth Sunday of Lent (Year A)*

### *John 9:1–41*

As he went along, he saw a man who had been blind from birth. His disciples asked him, 'Rabbi, who sinned, this man or his parents, that he was born blind?' Jesus replied, 'Neither he nor his parents sinned. He was born blind so that the works of God might be revealed in him.

'As long as day lasts
we must carry out the work of the one who sent me.
Night is coming when no one can work.
As long as I am in the world
I am the light of the world.'

Having said this, he spat on the ground, made a paste with the saliva, spread it on the man's eyes, and said to him, 'Go and wash in the Pool of Siloam' (which means 'Sent'). So he went off and washed and came back able to see.

His neighbours and people who had earlier seen that he was a beggar said, 'Is not this the man who used to sit and beg?' Some said, 'It is.' Others said, 'No, but he is like the man.' The man himself said, 'Yes, I am the one.' So they said to him, 'Then how were your eyes opened?' He answered, 'The man called Jesus made a paste, spread it on my eyes and said to me, "Go off and wash at Siloam." So I went and washed and could see.' They said to him, 'Where is he?' He answered, 'I do not know.'

They brought to the Pharisees the man who had been blind. It had been a Sabbath when Jesus made the paste and opened the man's eyes, so the Pharisees asked him again how he had come to see. He said to them, 'He put a paste on my eyes, and I washed, and I can see.' Then some of the Pharisees said, 'That man is not from God: he does not keep the Sabbath.' Others said, 'How can a sinner produce such signs?' And there was division among them. So they said to the blind man again,

'What have you to say about him – as it was your eyes he opened?' The man answered, 'He is a prophet.'

However, the Jews would not believe that the man had been blind and had come to see till they had sent for the parents of the man who had come to see and asked them, 'Is this man your son whom you say was born blind? If so, how can he now see?' His parents answered, 'We know that he is our son and that he was born blind, but how he can see, we do not know, nor who opened his eyes. Ask him. He is of age: he will speak for himself.' His parents said this because they were afraid of the Jews, for the Jews had already agreed that anyone who acknowledged Jesus as the Messiah should be banned from the synagogue. This was why his parents said, 'He is of age: ask him.'

So the Jews sent a second time for the man who had been blind and said to him, 'Give glory to God! We know that this man is a sinner.' He answered, 'Whether he is a sinner I don't

## FOURTH SUNDAY OF LENT (YEAR A)

know; one thing I do know is that though I was blind I can now see.' They said to him, 'What did he do to you? How did he open your eyes?' He replied, 'I have told you already and you did not listen. Why do you want to hear it again? Do you want to become his disciples yourselves?' At this they hurled abuse at him, 'You are his disciple, we are disciples of Moses. We know that God has spoken to Moses, but as for this man, we do not know where he comes from.' The man replied, 'The amazing thing is this: that you do not know where he comes from and he has opened my eyes! We know that God does not listen to sinners, but God does listen to someone who reveres God and does his will. Ever since the world began it is unheard of that anyone should open the eyes of someone born blind; if this man were not from God, he would not have been able to do anything.' They answered and said to him, 'You were born wholly in sin, and are you teaching us?' And they drove him out.

Jesus heard they had driven him out, and when he had found him he said, 'Do you believe in the Son of man?' He replied, 'And who is he, sir, that I may believe in him?' Jesus said to him, 'You have seen him, and he is the one speaking to you.' He said, 'Lord, I believe,' and worshipped him.

And Jesus said:

'For judgement I came into this world,
so that those who cannot see might see,
and those who can see might become blind.'

Hearing this, some of the Pharisees who were with him said to him, 'Surely we are not blind, are we?' Jesus replied:

'If you were blind
you would not be to blame,
but since you say,
"We can see," your guilt remains.'

Other readings: 1 Samuel 16:1, 6–7, 10–13   Psalm 22 (23)
Ephesians 5:8–14

## 64  FOURTH SUNDAY OF LENT (YEAR A)

ONCE AGAIN THIS WEEK we have a lengthy passage from the Gospel of John, the story of the man born blind. This is another story of a journey in faith, which invites us to consider our own journey. The words of Jesus at the very start (verse 5) give us the theme: Jesus is the light of the world. Like the man born blind, we too have the opportunity of seeing again, seeing with greater clarity.

Even in the opening verses the man has already had to defend the reality of the healing. Yes, he is indeed the man who was blind from birth and he has indeed been given his sight. As the chapter continues he bears witness to Jesus more and more strongly and more and more indignantly. In the end it is clear that there are none so blind as those who will not see. The religious leaders refuse to see that Jesus brings light into the world. They refuse to acknowledge their own blindness.

It may seem strange that we have the story of David's anointing as king in the first reading. This reminds us that, as we were given the light of faith in baptism, we were also anointed for God's service. St Paul tells the Christians of Ephesus in our second reading: 'You were darkness once, but now you are light in the Lord.'

*What might we learn from the courageous witness of the man born blind?*

*Am I to some extent still blind and unwilling to see?*

*We pray for those who are still seeking the light and discouraged by darkness.*

*We pray for all those to be baptised at Easter.*

---

# Fifth Sunday of Lent (Year A)

## John 11:1–45

There was a sick man named Lazarus of Bethany, the village of Mary and her sister, Martha. It was Mary, the sister of the sick man Lazarus, who anointed the Lord with ointment and wiped his feet with her hair. The sisters sent this message to Jesus, 'Lord, the one you love is sick.' On hearing this, Jesus said, "This sickness will not lead to death, but is for God's glory so that through it the Son of God may be glorified.'

## FIFTH SUNDAY OF LENT (YEAR A)

Jesus loved Martha and her sister and Lazarus, yet when he heard that he was sick he stayed where he was for two more days. Then after this he said to the disciples, 'Let us go back to Judaea.' The disciples said, 'Rabbi, just now the Jews were trying to stone you; are you going back there again?' Jesus replied:

'Are there not twelve hours in the day?
No one who walks in the daytime stumbles,
having the light of this world to see by;
anyone who walks around at night stumbles,
having no light as a guide.'

He said that and then added, 'Our friend Lazarus is at rest; I am going to wake him up.' The disciples said to him, 'Lord, if he is at rest he will be saved.' Jesus had been speaking of the death of Lazarus, but they thought that by 'rest' he meant sleep. So Jesus put it plainly, 'Lazarus has died; and for your sake I am glad I was not there, so that you may believe. But let us go to him.' Then Thomas – known as the Twin – said to the other disciples, 'Let us also go to die with him.'

On arriving, Jesus found that Lazarus had been in the tomb for four days already. Bethany is only about three kilometres from Jerusalem, and many Jews had come to Martha and Mary to comfort them about their brother. When Martha heard that Jesus was coming she went to meet him. Mary remained sitting in the house.

Martha said to Jesus, 'Lord, if you had been here, my brother would not have died, but even now I know that God will grant whatever you ask of him.' Jesus said to her, 'Your brother will rise again.' Martha said to him, 'I know he will rise again at the resurrection on the last day.' Jesus said to her:

'I am the resurrection and life.
Anyone who believes in me,
even though that person dies, will live,
and no one who lives and believes in me will ever die.
Do you believe this?'

She said, 'Yes, Lord. I believe that you are the Messiah, the Son of God, the one coming into this world.'

When she had said this, she went and called her sister Mary, saying quietly, 'The Master is here and is calling you.' Hearing this, Mary got up quickly and went to him. Jesus had not yet come into the village; he was still at the place where Martha had met him. The Jews who were in the house comforting Mary, seeing her get up quickly and go out, followed her, thinking that she was going to the tomb to weep there. When Mary came to where Jesus was, seeing him she fell at his feet, saying, 'Lord, if you had been here, my brother would not have died.' When Jesus saw her weeping, and the Jews who had come with her also, he was distressed in spirit, and profoundly moved. He said, 'Where have you laid him?' They said, 'Lord, come and see.' Jesus wept; and the Jews said, 'See how he loved him!' Some of them said, 'Could not he who opened the eyes of the blind man have prevented this man from dying?' Again inwardly distressed, Jesus reached the tomb: it was a cave, closed by a stone. Jesus said, 'Take the stone away.' Martha, the dead man's sister, said to him, 'Lord, there is already a stench; he has been dead for four days.' Jesus replied, 'Have I not told you that if you believe you will see the glory of God?' So they took the stone away. Then Jesus lifted up his eyes and said:

'Father, I thank you for hearing my prayer.
I myself knew that you hear me always,
but I speak
for the sake of all the crowd standing around me,
so that they may believe that you sent me.'

When he had said this, he cried in a loud voice, 'Lazarus, come out!' The dead man came out, his feet and hands bound with strips of material, and his face wrapped in a cloth. Jesus said to them, 'Unbind him, and let him go.'

Many of the Jews who had come to visit Mary, and had seen what he did, believed in him.

Other readings: Ezekiel 37:12–14   Psalm 129 (130)   Romans 8:8–11

THIS SUNDAY'S EXTENDED PASSAGE from the Gospel of John is the story of the raising of Lazarus. The words of Jesus to Martha in verse 25 give us the theme: Jesus is the resurrection and the life. No wonder he goes on later in the chapter to restore earthly life to Lazarus as a sign of the life to come.

Just as the healing of the man born blind was a 'work of God', inviting faith, similarly the raising of Lazarus shows the 'glory of God' (verse 40) and strengthens faith. All the so-called 'signs' in the Gospel of John do this (See John 2:11). The raising of Lazarus is the last and greatest of the signs. Both Martha and Mary are ready to witness that Jesus is 'the resurrection and the life'.

The story concludes with the statement that 'many believed in him' (verse 45). But this sign also provokes strong opposition from the religious leaders who plot to destroy Jesus. The one who gives life will have life torn from him in return.

In the other readings for today, too, there are clear pointers to the Resurrection to come. The prophet Ezekiel relays God's promise to give the people a new spirit and raise them from their graves. St Paul teaches the Romans about the life-giving Spirit of Christ, the Easter gift of the risen Jesus. The Psalmist cries 'out of the depths' to the Lord with whom there is 'mercy and fulness of redemption'. The prayer is heard by the God of life.

*How does this story prepare us for the celebration of the Easter mystery?*
*In what sense is this the greatest of the signs worked by Jesus?*
*We pray that we may understand and truly believe that God is the God of life.*
*We ask for the grace to live the time of Christ's Passion and death to the full.*

---

# *Passion (Palm) Sunday (Year A)*

## *Matthew 26:14 – 27:66*

Then one of the Twelve, the man called Judas Iscariot, went to the chief priests and said, 'What are you prepared to give me if I hand him over to you?' They settled with him for thirty silver pieces, and from then onwards he began to look for an opportunity to betray him.

Now on the first day of Unleavened Bread the disciples came to Jesus to say, 'Where do you want us to make the preparations for you to eat the Passover?' He said, 'Go to a certain man in the city and say to him, "The teacher says: My time is near. It is at your house that I am keeping Passover with my disciples."' The disciples did what Jesus told them and prepared the Passover. When evening came he was at table with the Twelve. And while they were eating he said, 'Amen I say to you, one of you is about to betray me.' They were greatly distressed and started asking him in turn, 'Not me, Lord, surely?' He answered, 'Someone who has dipped his hand into the dish with me will betray me. The Son of man is going to his fate, as it is written about him, but alas for that man by whom the Son of man is betrayed! It would have been better for that man if he had never been born!' Judas, who was to betray him, asked in his turn, 'Not me, Rabbi, surely?' Jesus answered, 'It is you who said it.'

Now as they were eating, Jesus took bread, and when he had said the blessing he broke it and giving it to the disciples he said, 'Take it and eat, this is my body.' Then taking a cup, after giving thanks he handed it to them saying, 'Drink from this, all of you, for this is my blood, the blood of the covenant, poured out for many for the forgiveness of sins. From now on, I tell you, I shall never again drink wine until the day I drink the new wine with you in the kingdom of my Father.'

Having sung the psalms they left for the Mount of Olives. Then Jesus said to them, 'You will all fall away from me tonight, for it is written, *I shall strike the shepherd and the sheep of the flock will be scattered*, but after I have been raised up I shall go before you into Galilee.' At this, Peter said to him, 'Even if all fall away from you, I will never fall away.' Jesus answered him, 'Amen I say to you, this very night, before the cock crows, you will deny me three times.' Peter said to him, 'Even if I have to die with you, I will never deny you.' And all the disciples spoke similarly.

Then Jesus came with them to a plot of land called Gethsemane; and he said to his disciples, 'Sit here while I go over there to pray.' He took Peter and the two sons of Zebedee with him. And he began to feel sadness and anguish. Then he said to them, 'My soul is sorrowful to the point of death. Wait here and stay awake with me.' And going on a little further he fell on his face and prayed, saying, 'My Father, if it is possible, let this cup pass from me. Only not as I want, but as you.'

He came back to the disciples and found them sleeping, and he said to Peter, 'So you had not the strength to stay awake with me for one hour? Stay awake, and pray not to enter into temptation. The spirit is eager, but the flesh is weak.' Again, a second time, he went away and prayed, saying, 'My Father, if this cup cannot pass by unless I drink it, your will be done!' And he came back again and found them sleeping, for their eyes were weighed down. Leaving them there, he went away again and prayed for the third time, repeating the same words. Then he came back to the disciples and said to them, 'Sleep on now and have your rest. Look, the hour is near when the Son of man is betrayed into the hands of sinners. Get up! Let us go! Look, my betrayer is near.'

And suddenly, while he was still speaking, Judas, one of the Twelve, came, and with him a large crowd armed with swords and clubs, sent by the chief priests and elders of the people. Now the traitor had given them a sign, saying, 'The one I kiss, he is the man. Take charge of him.' So he went up to Jesus at once and said, 'Greetings, Rabbi,' and kissed him. Jesus said to him, 'My friend, do what you are here for.' Then they came forward, laid hands on Jesus and took charge of him. And suddenly, one of the followers of Jesus grasped his sword and drew it; he struck the high priest's servant and cut off his ear. Then Jesus said, 'Put your sword back into its place, for all who draw the sword will die by the sword. Or do you think that I cannot appeal to my Father, who would promptly send more than twelve legions of angels to my defence? But then, how would the scriptures be fulfilled, which say that it must happen this way?' At that hour Jesus said to the crowds, 'Have you come out with swords and clubs to capture me as though I were a bandit? Day by day I sat teaching in the Temple and you did not lay hands on me.' Now all this happened so that the scriptures of the prophets should be fulfilled. Then all the disciples deserted him and ran away.

The men who had arrested Jesus led him off to Caiaphas the high priest, where the scribes and the elders were assembled. Peter followed him at a distance right to the courtyard of the high priest, and he went inside and sat down with the attendants to see what the end would be. The chief priests and the whole council were looking for false evidence against Jesus, on which they might have him executed. But they could not find any, though many false witnesses came forward. Eventually two came forward and said, 'This man said, "I have power to destroy the Temple of God and in three days build it up."' Then the high priest rose and said to him, 'Have you no answer to the evidence these men are bringing against you?' But Jesus was silent. And the high priest said to him, 'I put you on oath by the living God to tell us if you are the Messiah, the Son of God.' Jesus answered him, 'It is you who say it. Only, I tell you that from this time onward you will see *the Son of man seated at the right hand of the Power and coming on the clouds of heaven.*' Then the high priest tore his clothes and said, 'He has blasphemed. Why do we still need witnesses? See now! You have heard the blasphemy. What do you think?' They said in answer, 'He deserves to die.' Then they spat in his face and hit him with their fists, saying, 'Prophesy to us, Messiah! Who hit you?'

Meanwhile Peter was sitting outside in the courtyard, and a servant-girl came up to him saying, 'You, too, were with Jesus the Galilean.' But he denied it in front of them all, saying, 'I do not know or understand what you mean.' When he went out into the gateway another servant-girl saw him and said to the people there, 'This man was with Jesus the Nazarene.' And again, with an oath, he denied it, 'I do not know the man.' A little later the bystanders came up and said to Peter, 'You are certainly one of them too! Why, your accent gives you away.' Then he started cursing and swearing, 'I do not know the man.' And at once the cock crowed, and Peter remembered what Jesus had said, 'Before the cock crows you will deny me three times.' And he went outside and wept bitterly.

When morning came, all the chief priests and the elders

of the people met in council to bring about the death of Jesus. They bound him, took him off and handed him over to Pilate, the governor.

When Judas, his betrayer, saw that Jesus had been condemned, he was filled with remorse and took the thirty silver pieces back to the chief priests and elders, saying, 'I have sinned by betraying innocent blood.' They replied, 'What is that to us? See to it yourself.' And flinging down the silver pieces in the sanctuary he made off, and went and hanged himself. The chief priests picked up the silver pieces and said, 'It is not permissible to put this into the treasury; since it is blood-money.' So they discussed the matter and with it bought the potter's field as a graveyard for foreigners, and this is why the field has been called the Field of Blood till this day. The word spoken through the prophet Jeremiah was then fulfilled: *And they took the thirty silver pieces, the sum at which the precious One was priced by the children of Israel, and they gave them for the potter's field, just as the Lord directed me.*

Jesus, then, was brought before the governor, and the governor put to him this question, 'Are you the king of the Jews?' Jesus replied, 'You say so.' But when he was accused by the chief priests and the elders he did not answer. Pilate then said to him, 'Do you not hear how many accusations they are bringing against you?' But he did not answer a single word to him, so that the governor was amazed.

At festival time it was the governor's practice to release a prisoner for the people, anyone they chose. Now they had then a notorious prisoner called Barabbas. So when they had gathered, Pilate said to them, 'Which do you want me to release for you, Barabbas, or Jesus who is called the Messiah?' For Pilate knew it was out of jealousy that they had handed him over.

Now as he was seated in the chair of judgement, his wife sent him a message, 'Have nothing to do with that righteous man; I have been extremely upset today by a dream that I had about him.' The chief priests and the elders, however, had persuaded the crowds to ask for the release of Barabbas and the execution of Jesus. So when the governor spoke and asked them, 'Which of the two do you want me to release for you?' they said, 'Barabbas.' Pilate said to them, 'What, then, am I to do with Jesus who is called the Messiah?' They all said, 'Let him be crucified!' He asked, 'What evil has he done?' But they shouted all the more, 'Let him be crucified!' Then Pilate, seeing that he was making no impression, but rather that a riot was imminent, took some water, washed his hands in front of the crowd and said, 'I am innocent of this man's blood. You see to it.' And the whole people shouted back, 'Let his blood be on us and on our children!' Then he released Barabbas for them. After having Jesus scourged, he handed him over to be crucified.

Then the governor's soldiers took Jesus with them into the Praetorium and collected the whole cohort round him. And they stripped him and put a scarlet cloak round him, and having twisted some thorns into a crown they put this on his head and placed a reed in his right hand. To make fun of him they knelt to him saying, 'Hail, king of the Jews!' And they spat at him and took the reed and struck him on the head. And when they had mocked him, they took off the cloak and dressed him in his own clothes and led him away to crucifixion.

On their way out, they came across a man from Cyrene, called Simon, and enlisted him to carry his cross. When they had reached a place called Golgotha, which is called the place of the skull, they gave him wine to drink mixed with gall, which he tasted but refused to drink. When they had crucified him they shared out his clothing by casting lots, and then, sitting down, they guarded him there. And they placed above his head the charge against him; it read: 'This is Jesus, the King of the Jews.' Then they crucified two bandits with him, one on his right and one on his left. The passers-by jeered at him, shaking their heads and saying, 'You who destroy the Temple and in three days rebuild it, save yourself, if you are God's son, and come down from the cross!' The chief priests with the scribes and elders mocked him in the same way, with the words, 'He saved others; he cannot save himself. He is the king of Israel; let him come down from the cross now, and we will believe in him. He has put his trust in God; now let God rescue him if he wants him. For he said, "I am God's son."' In the same way even the bandits who were crucified with him taunted him.

From noon onwards there was darkness over all the land until mid-afternoon. And at that time, Jesus cried out in a loud voice, '*Eli, eli, lama sabachthani?*' that is, '*My God, my God, why have you forsaken me?*' When some of the bystanders there heard this, they said, 'He is calling on Elijah,' and one of them at once ran to get a sponge which he filled with vinegar and, putting it on a reed, gave it him to drink. But the rest of them said, 'Wait! Let us see if Elijah comes to save him.' But Jesus, again crying out in a loud voice, yielded up his spirit.

And suddenly, the veil of the sanctuary was torn in two from top to bottom, the earth quaked, the rocks were split, the tombs opened and the bodies of many holy people rose from the dead, and these, after his resurrection, came out of the tombs, entered the holy city and appeared to a number of people. The centurion, together with the others guarding Jesus, had seen the earthquake and all that was taking place, and they were terrified and said, 'In truth this man was son of God.'

And many women were there, watching from a distance, the same women who had followed Jesus from Galilee and looked after him. Among them were Mary of Magdala, Mary the mother of James and Joseph, and the mother of Zebedee's sons.

When it was evening, there came a rich man of Arimathaea, called Joseph, who had himself become a disciple of Jesus. This man went to Pilate and asked for the body of Jesus. Then Pilate ordered it to be handed over. So Joseph took the body, wrapped it in a clean linen cloth, and put it in his own new tomb which he had hewn in the rock. Then he rolled a large stone to the doorway of the tomb and went away. Now Mary of Magdala and the other Mary were there, sitting opposite the sepulchre. Next day, that is, when Preparation Day was over, the chief priests and the Pharisees gathered before Pilate and said to him, 'Sir, we recall that this deceiver said, while he was still alive, "After three days I shall rise again." Therefore give the order to have the sepulchre kept secure until the third day, for fear his disciples come and steal him away and tell the people, "He has been raised from the dead." This last fraud would be worse than the first.' Pilate said to them, 'You have a guard; go and make all as secure as you know how.' So they went and made the sepulchre secure, putting seals on the stone with the guard.

**Other readings: Isaiah 50:4–7   Psalm 21 (22)   Philippians 2:6–11**

THE STORY OF THE Passion of Christ is solemnly read as we begin Holy Week. This evangelist follows Mark in recording the opening words of the psalm as Jesus' last words, and thus shows how deep is the anguish of Jesus, the good man abused by evil-doers. The words of Jesus are misunderstood by the bystanders, who attempt to prolong his life by offering him vinegar. Matthew tells us that at his death Jesus freely gives up his spirit.

The evangelist, who has already spoken of darkness over the whole earth, narrates apocalyptic happenings at the death of Jesus. But the death of the Son of God also heralds new life, not only for Jesus, but also for the saints who sleep in death. Furthermore, Matthew has those guarding Jesus join the centurion in a chorus of awe-struck faith at the death of Jesus. The evangelist implies that Jesus brings new life both to Jewish saints and to gentile soldiers, in other words to all. The faithful women from Galilee, who have served Jesus throughout his ministry, stand by as witnesses to these awesome events.

*What are the striking features of the story of the Passion as told by Matthew?*
*Take time this week to read again the whole of Matthew's account of the death of Christ.*
*We pray that our Holy Week will prepare us for the gift of new life at Easter.*
*We join Christians throughout the world in living these holy days to the full.*

# YEAR B

## *First Sunday of Lent (Year B)*

### Mark 1:12–15

And at once the Spirit drove him into the desert and he was in the desert for forty days, being put to the test by Satan. He was with the wild animals, and the angels looked after him.

After John had been arrested, Jesus went into Galilee, proclaiming the gospel from God and saying, 'The time is fulfilled, and the kingdom of God has drawn near. Repent and believe in the gospel.'

**Other readings: Genesis 9:8–15   Psalm 24 (25)   1 Peter 3:18–22**

IT IS AN ANCIENT custom in the Church that the story of the temptation of Jesus in the desert should be read on the first Sunday of Lent. Jesus spent forty days in the wilderness. At the beginning of the forty days of Lent the Church always puts before us his time of solitude.

The temptation of Jesus is recounted in the three gospels known as 'synoptics', the gospels of Matthew, Mark and Luke. While Matthew and Luke give an extended version of the tradition, telling us that Jesus fasted for forty days and reporting a dialogue between Jesus and the devil, Mark simply gives the outline of the story.

Jesus has just received baptism from John in the river Jordan and he is filled with the Spirit. This same Spirit drives him into the wilderness, the place of desolation and loneliness, thought to be the habitat of evil spirits. Jesus' forty days in the desert remind us of the forty-day journey of the prophet Elijah to the holy mountain where his call is renewed in the 'still, small voice'. We may even compare Jesus' stay in the wilderness with the forty years of wandering by Moses and the people.

The central statement is that Jesus was tempted. To be tempted is the fate of all human beings. That Jesus was tempted shows his humanity. He was 'like us in all things but sin'. He did not give way to temptation. Mark balances his statement about temptation with the laconic declarations 'he was with the wild animals' and 'the angels looked after him'. The evangelist shows that this Son of Man is at peace with all creation and cared for by the providence of the Father.

Our gospel reading concludes with a reminder of Jesus' mission, to preach the 'gospel from God', to announce that the time has come and that the kingdom is approaching. These statements of Jesus have a particular resonance as we begin the season of Lent, a time of self-examination and self-denial. We are invited to welcome God's special time of blessing and the coming of the kingdom into our lives.

*How does the story of the temptation enrich my understanding of the humanity of Jesus?*
*How does this story strike me as I begin Lent?*
*Let us pray for the Church as we begin this season of fasting and prayer.*
*Let us pray for the hungry, and let us work for a fairer distribution of the world's goods.*

---

# *Second Sunday of Lent (Year B)*

## *Mark 9:2–10*

Six days later, Jesus took with him Peter and James and John and led them up a high mountain on their own by themselves. In their presence he was transfigured: his clothes became brilliantly white, whiter than any earthly bleacher could make them. Elijah appeared to them with Moses; and they were talking to Jesus. Then Peter spoke to Jesus, 'Rabbi,' he said, 'it is wonderful for us to be here; so let us make three shelters, one for you, one for Moses and one for Elijah.' He did not know what to say; they were so frightened. And a cloud came, covering them in shadow; and from the cloud came a voice, 'This is my Son, the Beloved. Listen to him.' Then suddenly, when they looked round, they saw no one with them any more but only Jesus.

As they were coming down from the mountain he instructed them to tell no one what they had seen, except

# SECOND SUNDAY OF LENT (YEAR B)

when the Son of man had risen from the dead. And they kept the matter to themselves, though they puzzled what 'rising from the dead' could mean.

**Other readings: Genesis 22:1-2, 9-13, 15-18   Psalm 115 (116)
Romans 8:31-34**

IT IS AN ANCIENT tradition that the story of the Transfiguration of Jesus is read on the Second Sunday of Lent. This mysterious story tells of a strange transformation in the appearance of Jesus which profoundly affects the three chosen disciples. In addition, they see a vision of Moses and Elijah and they hear the voice of God.

To understand this gospel and its place in the early days of Lent we need to observe that this experience comes as Jesus begins his journey from Galilee to Jerusalem. All three 'synoptic' gospels of Matthew, Mark and Luke highlight this journey of Jesus and relate how, even though he foresees his death and resurrection, he remains determined to go to Jerusalem where he will face arrest, trial and crucifixion. The disciples accompany him in a state of reluctance and bewilderment.

The strange vision gives the disciples a glimpse of the future which lies beyond suffering and death. Both Moses and Elijah are said in ancient writings to have been taken up to live in the presence of God. Their testimony confirms the hope of the resurrection.

God's voice recalls the baptism scene as once again Jesus is proclaimed to be the beloved Son of God. There the Father had commended him as Jesus, the sinless one, began his ministry by sharing in the baptism 'for the forgiveness of sins'. Now the Father again approves of the Son as he courageously begins his journey to the place of martyrdom.

*What does this story teach you as the season of Lent progresses?*
*What is the most important feature of the story in your understanding?*
*Let us pray for all Christians that we may keep sight of the hope of resurrection.*
*Let us pray for all those preparing to be baptised at Easter.*

## Third Sunday of Lent (Year B)

### John 2:13-25

The time of the Jewish Passover was near and Jesus went up to Jerusalem. In the Temple he found people selling cattle and sheep and doves, and the money-changers sitting there. Making a whip out of cords, he began to drive them all out of the Temple, both sheep and cattle, scattered the money-changers' coins, overturned their tables and said to the dove-sellers, 'Take all this away from here and stop making my Father's house a market-house.' Then his disciples remembered that it had been written, *I am eaten up with zeal for your house.* The Jews in reply said, 'What sign can you show us for doing this?' Jesus answered, 'Destroy this Temple, and in three days I will raise it up.' The Jews replied, 'It took forty-six years to build this Temple: are you going to raise it up in three days?' But he was speaking about the Temple that was his body. When he had been raised from the dead, his disciples remembered that he had said this, and they believed the scripture and the words that he had spoken.

While he was in Jerusalem for the festival of the Passover many believed in his name because they saw the signs that he did, but Jesus did not trust himself to them, since he knew all people. He needed no witness about anyone; he himself knew what was in everyone.

**Other readings: Exodus 20:1-17   Psalm 18 (19)   1 Corinthians 1:22-25**

ONE OF THE FEATURES of the Gospel of John is that Jesus is frequently to be found in Jerusalem. The story about the 'cleansing of the temple' is placed by this evangelist at the start of Jesus' ministry, while in the other gospels it comes as a trigger for Jesus' arrest. The dialogue with the Jews about 'the Temple that was his body' is only found in John's gospel.

Jesus comes to bring a new age, a new time, a new form of worship. He is the Word among us. He reveals the way to God. It is not therefore surprising that when Jesus causes disruption in the temple the conversation shifts to the significance of the temple, and to the significance of his coming.

Jesus speaks in terms which are not immediately clear. Later, after his death and resurrection, the full import of his words will be apparent. Just as the temple is soon to be destroyed, so too the body of Jesus will be brought to death. But the future lies in the new life of the resurrection. Despite this enigma the evangelist tells us that many in Jerusalem came to believe in Jesus' name. From the start his words and person attracted those with the courage to see and understand.

*What does the cleansing of the temple symbolise?*
*Is it helpful to see Jesus as the 'new temple'?*
*Let us pray that our Lenten journey will be richly blessed.*
*Let us pray for the Jewish people, our elder brothers and sisters in the faith.*

---

# *Fourth Sunday of Lent (Year B)*

## *John 3:14–21*
Jesus said to Nicodemus:

'As Moses lifted up the snake in the desert,
so must the Son of man be lifted up
so that everyone who believes in him
may have eternal life.
For God loved the world so much
that he gave his only-begotten Son,
so that everyone who believes in him
may not perish but may have eternal life.
For God sent his Son into the world
not to judge the world,
but so that the world might be saved through him.
One who believes in him will not be judged;
but whoever does not believe is judged already,
for not believing in the name of God's only-begotten Son.
And the judgement is this:
that the light has come into the world
and people loved darkness rather than light

because their deeds were evil.
And indeed, everybody who does wrong
hates the light and does not come to the light,
so that such actions may not be examined.
But whoever does the truth comes to the light,
so that it may be clearly seen
that this person's works have been done in God.'

**Other readings: 2 Chronicles 36:14–16, 19–23    Psalm 136 (137)
Ephesians 2:4–10**

DURING LENT WE FREQUENTLY turn to the Gospel of John, for it contains a rich commentary on the events of the life of Jesus. In the conversation between Jesus and Nicodemus in chapter 3 of the gospel Jesus explains privately to a Jew the significance of the coming of the Son of God. Nicodemus was described at the beginning of this chapter as a teacher. This teacher is willing to be taught by Jesus. The evangelist will not tell us whether Nicodemus accepts the teaching or not. After some early exchanges, we then hear no more words of Nicodemus, but only the teaching of Jesus.

The raising up of the Son of God speaks both of his death on the cross and of his resurrection. His death is considered glorious. It leads inevitably to resurrection and triumph. The coming of the Son and his self-giving in death and resurrection are the clearest proof of the love of God for the world. People are called to respond in faith. As St Paul teaches, it is by God's grace that we are saved, through faith. God saves us if only we will allow it. To refuse Christ knowingly is to refuse salvation.

The symbol of light is common in John's gospel. From the very start of the gospel we learnt that the Light came into the world to challenge the darkness, and that the darkness could not overpower the Light. The theme of light returns here. Nicodemus comes to Jesus during the night. Like him we are free to embrace the light or to prefer darkness. Reference to 'the truth' is also frequent in John's gospel. We will live by the truth, if we allow Jesus to lead us ever deeper into that truth.

*Where do you need the light to shine in your life?*
*What does 'doing the truth' mean?*
*Let us pray for those who are discovering the truth of Christ.*
*Let us pray for those who struggle to see and accept the light.*

---

# *Fifth Sunday of Lent (Year B)*

## *John 12:20-33*

Among those who went up to worship at the festival were some Greeks. These approached Philip, who was from Bethsaida in Galilee, and put this request to him, 'Sir, we would like to see Jesus.' Philip went to tell Andrew, and Andrew and Philip together went to tell Jesus.

Jesus replied to them:

'Now the hour has come
for the Son of man to be glorified.
Amen, Amen I say to you,
unless a wheat grain falls into the earth and dies,
it remains only a single grain;
but if it dies it bears much fruit
Anyone who loves life loses it;
anyone who hates life in this world
will keep it for eternal life.
Whoever serves me, must follow me,
and my servant will be with me wherever I am.
Whoever serves me, my Father will honour.
Now my soul is troubled.
What shall I say:
Father, save me from this hour?
But it is for this very reason
that I have come to this hour.
Father, glorify your name!'

A voice came from heaven, 'I have glorified it, and I will again glorify it.'

The crowd standing by, who heard this, said it was thunder; others said, 'An angel has spoken to him.' Jesus answered, 'This voice came not for my sake, but for yours.
'Now is the judgement of this world,
now the ruler of this world will be driven out.
And when I am lifted up from the earth,
I shall draw all people to myself.'

Saying this he indicated the kind of death he would die.

**Other readings: Jeremiah 31:31–34   Psalm 50 (51)   Hebrews 5:7–9**

One of the features of the Gospel of John is that Jesus is frequently in Jerusalem. This particular episode comes as his ministry ends. The following chapters will tell of the washing of the disciples' feet and report the words of Jesus to the disciples on the night before he died. The story of the Passion will then begin. This text is therefore particularly apt as we draw closer to Holy Week.

The arrival of some Greeks shows how the ministry of Jesus breaks the bounds of Judaism. Their coming allows Jesus to speak of his hour and his willingness to give his life for all. The seed which must die to produce a harvest is a powerful image of his death. A voice is heard from the cloud, as at the Transfiguration in the other gospels, but here it speaks of the 'glory' that will come to Jesus for giving up his life. Once again, as in earlier chapters, Jesus speaks of being lifted up. It is in his death and resurrection that he draws all people to himself, both Jew and Greek.

*Do I still desire to 'see Jesus' and learn about him?*
*Whom have I brought to Jesus recently?*
*Let us pray for the mission of the Church to the nations of the world.*
*Let us pray for a deeper faith and love as we approach the 'hour' of*
    *Jesus in Holy Week.*

## *Passion (Palm) Sunday (Year B)*

### *Mark 14:1 – 15:47*

It was two days before the Passover and the feast of Unleavened Bread, and the chief priests and the scribes were looking for a way to arrest Jesus by some trick and kill him. For they said, 'Not during the feast, or there may be a disturbance among the people.'

When he was at Bethany in the house of Simon the leper, while he was at table a woman came in with an alabaster jar of very costly ointment, pure nard. She broke the jar and poured the ointment on his head. There were some who said to one another indignantly, 'Why has this waste of ointment happened? This ointment could have been sold for over three hundred denarii and the money given to the poor'; and they were angry with her. But Jesus said, 'Leave her alone. Why are you upsetting her? She has done me a good service. You have the poor with you always, and you can benefit them whenever you wish, but me you will not always have. She has done what she could: she has anointed my body beforehand for its burial. Amen I say to you, wherever throughout all the world the gospel is proclaimed, what she has done will also be told, in remembrance of her.'

Judas Iscariot, one of the Twelve, went off to the chief priests so that he might hand Jesus over to them. Hearing it, they were delighted, and promised to give him money; and he began to look for a way of betraying him at an opportune time.

On the first day of Unleavened Bread, when they used to sacrifice the Passover lamb, his disciples said to him, 'Where do you want us to go and make the preparations for you to eat the Passover?' So he sent two of his disciples, saying to them, 'Go into the city and someone will meet you carrying a pitcher of water. Follow him, and wherever he enters say to the owner of the house, "The teacher says: Where is the room where I may eat the Passover with my disciples?" He will show you a large upper room ready set out. Make the preparations for us there.' The disciples set out and went to the city and found everything as he had told them, and prepared the Passover.

When evening came he arrived with the Twelve. And while they were at table eating, Jesus said, 'Amen I say to you, one of you is about to betray me, one of you *eating with me*.' They were distressed and said to him, one after another, 'Not me, surely?' He said to them, 'It is one of the Twelve, one who is dipping into the same dish with me. For the Son of man is going to his fate, as it is written about him, but alas for that man by whom the Son of man is betrayed! Better for that man if he had never been born.'

And as they were eating he took bread, and when he had said the blessing he broke it, gave it to them and said, 'Take it, this is my body.' Then taking a cup, after giving thanks he gave it to them, and all drank from it, and he said to them, 'This is my blood of the covenant, poured out for many. Amen I say to you, I shall never again drink wine until that day when I drink new wine in the kingdom of God.'

Having sung the psalms they left for the Mount of Olives. And Jesus said to them, 'You will all fall away, for it is written: *I shall strike the shepherd and the sheep will be scattered*; however, after I have been raised up I shall go before you into Galilee.' Peter said, 'Even if all fall away, I will not.' And Jesus said to him, 'Amen I say to you, today, this very night, before the cock crows twice, you will deny me three times.' But he repeated still more strongly, 'Even if I have to die with you, I will never deny you.' And they all said the same.

They came to a plot of land called Gethsemane, and he said to his disciples, 'Sit here while I pray.' Then he took Peter and James and John with him. And he began to feel dismay and anguish. And he said to them, 'My soul is deeply sorrowful to the point of death. Wait here, and stay awake.' And going on a little further he began falling to the ground and prayed that, if it were possible, this hour might pass away from him. And he said, '*Abba*, Father! For you everything is possible. Take this cup away from me. Yet not what I want but what you want.' He came and found them sleeping, and he said to Peter, 'Simon, are you asleep? Had you not the strength to stay awake one hour? Stay awake and pray not to enter into temptation. The spirit is eager, but flesh is weak.' Again he went away and prayed, saying the same words. And once more he came and found them sleeping, for their eyes were weighed down; and they did not know how they should answer him. He came a third time and said to them, 'Sleep on and have your rest. Enough! The hour has come. See, the Son of man is being betrayed into the hands of sinners. Get up! Let us go! See, my betrayer is not far away.'

And at once, while he was still speaking, Judas, one of the Twelve, came up, and with him a crowd with swords and clubs from the chief priests and the scribes and the elders. Now the traitor had arranged a sign with them saying, 'The one I will kiss, he is the man. Take charge of him, and lead him away securely.' So when he came, he went up to Jesus at once and said, 'Rabbi!' and kissed him. The others laid hands on him and took charge of him. Then one of the bystanders drew his sword and struck out at the high priest's servant and cut off his ear.

Then Jesus replied saying, 'Have you come out with swords and clubs to capture me as though I were a bandit? Day by day I was among you teaching in the Temple and you did not lay hands on me. But let the scriptures be fulfilled.' And they all deserted him and fled. A young man was following him with nothing on but a linen cloth. They caught hold of him, but he left the cloth behind and fled naked.

They led Jesus off to the high priest; and all the chief priests and the elders and the scribes assembled. Peter had followed him at a distance, right into the courtyard of the high priest, and was sitting with the attendants warming himself at the fire.

The chief priests and the whole council were looking for evidence against Jesus in order to put him to death. But they could not find any, for many gave false evidence against him, but their evidence did not agree. Some stood up and gave this false evidence against him, 'We heard him say, "I will destroy this Temple made by human hands, and in three days build another, not made by human hands."' But even so their evidence did not agree. The high priest then stood up before the whole council and questioned Jesus saying, 'Have you no answer at all to the evidence they are bringing against you?' But he was silent and made no answer at all. Again the high priest questioned him saying, 'Are you the Messiah, the Son of the Blessed One?' Jesus said, 'I am; and you will see the *Son of man seated at the right hand of the Power and coming with the clouds of heaven.*' Then the high priest tore his clothes and said, 'Why do we still need witnesses? You heard the blasphemy. What is your opinion?' They all condemned him as deserving death.

Some of them started to spit at him, cover his face, buffet him and say 'Prophesy!' And the attendants took him over, slapping him in the face.

While Peter was down below in the courtyard, one of the high priest's servant-girls came up. She saw Peter warming himself there, she stared at him and said, 'You were with Jesus, the man from Nazareth, too.' But he denied it saying, 'I do not know, and do not understand what you are talking about.' And he went out into the forecourt, and a cock crowed. And seeing him the servant-girl again started saying to the bystanders, 'This man is one of them.' But again he denied it. A little later the bystanders themselves said to Peter, 'You certainly are one of them! You are a Galilean too.' But he started cursing and swearing, 'I do not know this man you are talking about.' And at once the cock crowed for the second time, and Peter recalled how Jesus had said to him, 'Before the cock crows twice, you will deny me three times.' And he burst into tears.

And at once in the morning, the chief priests, together with the elders and scribes and the rest of the assembly, having prepared a plan and bound Jesus, took him off and handed him over to Pilate. Pilate asked him, 'Are you the king of the Jews?' He replied, 'You say so.' And the chief priests brought many accusations against him. Pilate questioned him again, 'Do you make no reply at all? See how many accusations they are bringing against you!' But Jesus made no further reply, so that Pilate was amazed.

At festival time Pilate used to release a prisoner for them, any one they asked for. Now someone called Barabbas was then in prison with the rebels who had committed murder during the uprising. When the crowd went up and began to ask Pilate to do the customary favour for them, Pilate answered them, 'Do you want me to release for you the king of the Jews?' For he realised it was out of spite that the chief priests had handed Jesus over. The chief priests, however, stirred up the crowd so that he should release Barabbas for them instead. Then Pilate spoke to them again, 'What, then, am I to do with the man you call king of the Jews?' They shouted back, 'Crucify him!' Pilate asked them, 'What evil has he done?' But they shouted all the more, 'Crucify him!' So Pilate, anxious to satisfy the crowd, released Barabbas for them and, after having Jesus scourged, handed him over to be crucified.

The soldiers led him away to the inner part of the palace, that is, the Praetorium, and called the whole cohort together. They clothed him in purple, twisted some thorns into a crown and put it on him. And they began saluting him, 'Hail, king of the Jews!' They struck his head with a reed and spat on him; and kneeling down they worshipped him. And when they had mocked him, they took off the purple, dressed him in his own clothes and led him out to crucify him.

They enlisted a passer-by, Simon of Cyrene, father of Alexander and Rufus, who was coming from the country, to carry his cross. They brought Jesus to the place called Golgotha, which means the place of the skull.

They offered him wine mixed with myrrh, but he did not take it. Then they crucified him, and *shared out his clothes by casting lots* to decide what each should take. It was midmorning when they crucified him. The inscription of the charge against him read, 'The King of the Jews'. And they crucified two bandits with him, one on his right and one on his left. The passers-by jeered at him, shaking their heads and saying, 'Aha! You who destroy the Temple and rebuild it in three days, save yourself! Come down from the cross!' The chief priests and the scribes mocked him among themselves in the same way saying, 'He saved others, he cannot save himself. Let the Messiah, the king of Israel, come down from the cross now, so that we may see it and believe.' Those who were crucified with him also taunted him.

When noon came there was darkness over the whole land until mid-afternoon. And at that time Jesus cried out in a loud voice, '*Eloi, eloi, lama sabachthani?*' which means, '*My God, my God, why have you forsaken me?*' When some of the bystanders heard, they said, 'Listen, he is calling Elijah.' And someone ran and soaked a sponge in vinegar and, putting it on a stick, gave it to him to drink saying, 'Wait! Let us see if Elijah comes to take him down.' But Jesus let out a loud cry and breathed his last. And the curtain of the Temple was torn in two from top to bottom. The centurion, who was standing opposite him, seeing that he had breathed his last, said, 'In truth this man was Son of God.'

There were some women watching from a distance. Among them were Mary of Magdala, Mary who was the mother of James the younger and Joset, and Salome. These used to follow him and look after him when he was in Galilee. And many other women were there who had come up to Jerusalem with him.

Now as soon as evening came, since it was Preparation Day – that is, the day before the Sabbath – Joseph of Arimathaea, a respected member of the council, who was himself awaiting the kingdom of God, went boldly to Pilate and asked for the body of Jesus. Pilate, surprised if he was already dead, summoned the centurion and asked if he had been long dead. Having been assured of this by the centurion, he granted the corpse to Joseph. Joseph bought a linen cloth, and taking him down from the cross, wrapped him in the shroud, laid him in a tomb which had been hewn out of the rock and rolled a stone against the doorway of the tomb. Mary of Magdala and Mary the mother of Joset were watching where he was laid.

**Other readings: Isaiah 50:4–7   Psalm 21 (22)   Philippians 2:6–11**

THIS STORY OF THE Passion of Jesus according to Mark is punctuated by the evangelist's references to the time of day. Jesus is crucified 'at the third hour'. Roman reckoning of day-time hours began with 6 a.m. so this is 9 a.m. The darkness over the earth begins at noon. Jesus 'breathes his last' at 3 o'clock, the traditional time for recalling the death of Christ.

Three groups mock Jesus. Anonymous passers-by taunt Jesus

by referring to his words about the temple. The chief-priests and scribes mock Jesus, who 'saved others, but cannot save himself'. They also ridicule him with his supposed claims to be the Messiah. Finally, Mark tells us that 'those who were crucified with him also taunted him'. This evangelist appears to know nothing about the 'good thief'.

Jesus' final words are words of abandonment. The Son of God, who comes to share our life and give his life for us, drinks the cup of suffering to the depth out of love for his brothers and sisters. And thus he dies.

*What are the memorable features of Mark's story of the death of Jesus?*
*Take time this week to read again the complete story of the death of Jesus as told by Mark.*
*Let us enter fully into the events of Holy Week so that we may be renewed in Christ's resurrection.*
*We pray that the self-giving love of Christ for all will change minds and hearts.*

# YEAR C

## *First Sunday of Lent (Year C)*

### Luke 4:1-13

Filled with the Holy Spirit, Jesus left the Jordan and was led by the Spirit into the desert, for forty days being put to the test by the devil. During that time he ate nothing at all and when they were over he was hungry. Then the devil said to him, 'If you are Son of God, tell this stone to become a loaf.' But Jesus replied to him, 'Scripture says:

*A human does not live on bread alone.'*

Then, leading him to a height, the devil showed him in a moment of time all the kingdoms of the world and said to him, 'I will give you all this power and their splendour, for it has been handed over to me, and I give it to anyone I wish. If you, then, worship me, it shall all be yours.' But Jesus answered him, 'It is written:

*You shall worship the Lord your God, him alone shall you serve.'*

Then he led him to Jerusalem and set him on the parapet of the Temple and said to him, 'If you are Son of God throw yourself down from here, for it is written:

*He has given his angels orders about you, to guard you,* and that, *They will carry you in their arms in case you trip on a stone.'*

But Jesus answered him, 'It is said:

*Do not put the Lord your God to the test.'*

Having finished every way of putting him to the test, the devil left him, until the opportune moment.

**Other readings: Deuteronomy 26:4–10    Psalm 90 (91)    Romans 10:8–13**

IT IS AN ANCIENT tradition that we read the gospel of the temptation of Jesus on the first Sunday of Lent. There is the obvious connection that Jesus spends forty days in the wilderness, but there are deeper reasons. In each of the synoptic gospels we are told how, before his ministry begins, Jesus, filled with the Spirit, encounters the spirit of evil. It is what his ministry is all about. It is what our lives are all about. To overcome evil with goodness is the constant challenge of the gospel.

In the longer narratives in Matthew and Luke we are given what amounts to a profound reflection on the nature of temptation. To use God-given powers for selfish ends is a temptation rife in our modern times. To worship the source of evil recalls our modern confusion about what is morally good and morally bad. To put God to the test is similarly familiar. Jesus withstands each of these tests. Our gospel ends with the departure of the devil 'until the opportune moment'. Luke knows that the critical time will come at Calvary.

*Which temptations are present in my life and how should I withstand them?*

*Do I share the moral confusion of the present time?*

*Let us pray for honesty in order to change our attitudes and our behaviour.*

*Let us pray for the strength of God's Spirit to put our lives to right this Lent.*

---

# *Second Sunday of Lent (Year C)*

## *Luke 9:28–36*

Now about eight days after these sayings, taking Peter, John and James with him he went up the mountain to pray. And it happened that, as he was praying, the aspect of his face was changed and his clothing became dazzling white. And suddenly there were two men talking to him; they were Moses and Elijah appearing in glory, and they were speaking of his departure which he was to accomplish in Jerusalem. Peter and his companions were heavy with sleep, but when they were fully awake they saw his glory and the two men standing with him. As these were leaving him, Peter said to Jesus, 'Master, it is wonderful for us to be here; so let us make three shelters, one for you, one for Moses and one for Elijah,' not knowing what he was saying. While he was saying this, a cloud came and covered them with shadow; and as they went into the cloud the disciples were afraid. And a voice came from the cloud saying, 'This is my Son, the Chosen One. Listen to him.' And after the voice had spoken, Jesus was found alone. They themselves kept silence and, in those days, told no one what they had seen.

**Other readings: Genesis 15:5–12, 17–18   Psalm 26 (27)**
**Philippians 3:17–4:1**

AFTER THE STARK READING about the temptations of Jesus in last Sunday's gospel we hear the gospel of the Transfiguration on the second Sunday of Lent. The story, found in the gospels of Matthew,

Mark and Luke, is an extraordinary one, narrating a mysterious event which deeply struck the disciples.

Jesus is seen transformed by three of his disciples. His face is changed and he wears brilliant clothing, which suggests the life of the resurrection. Moses and Elijah are with him. These two great figures from the Scriptures were believed, after many trials, to have been taken to the presence of God. No burial-place of Moses was ever found. Elijah, it was believed, had been taken up to heaven in a chariot. Luke says that they speak with Jesus of his 'departure' or 'exodus', his leaving this world to return to the Father, that journey through suffering and death which they too have known. It is as if they provide encouragement as Jesus begins his journey to Jerusalem and to death.

The story of the Transfiguration is very elaborate. We read it in Lent both to focus on the triumph of Jesus beyond the cross, and to hear again the words: 'This is my Son, the Chosen One. Listen to him!' Above all it invites us to accompany Jesus as he journeys through death to the life of the resurrection, a life which God prepares for us too, a life we can scarcely imagine.

*What message can we take from the gospel of the Transfiguration in times of trial?*
*Do I really listen to the words of the Son, found in the Holy Scriptures?*
*We pray for courage as we face the difficulties of life.*
*We pray for the freedom to allow the hope of the resurrection to transform our lives.*

---

# *Third Sunday of Lent (Year C)*

## *Luke 13:1-9*

On this occasion some people were present who told him about the Galileans whose blood Pilate had mingled with that of their sacrifices. In reply he said to them, 'Do you suppose that these Galileans were worse sinners than all other Galileans, that this should have happened to them? No, I tell you, but unless you repent you will all perish as they did. Or those eighteen on whom the tower at Siloam fell, killing them? Do you suppose that they were more guilty

# THIRD SUNDAY OF LENT (YEAR C)

than all the other people living in Jerusalem? No; but unless you repent you will all perish as they did.'

He told this parable, 'A man had a fig tree planted in his vineyard, and he came looking for fruit on it but found none. He said to the gardener, "For three years now I have been coming to look for fruit on this fig tree and finding none. Cut it down: why should it be taking up the ground?" In reply he said, "Sir, leave it just this year and give me time to dig round it and manure it: it may bear fruit next year; if not, then you can cut it down."'

**Other readings: Exodus 3:1-8, 13-15   Psalm 102 (103)
1 Corinthians 10:1-6, 10-12**

THIS GOSPEL READING CONTAINS material found in no other gospel which raises crucial questions about the justice of God and the need for repentance. We frequently hear about human suffering, suffering inflicted by other people or resulting from 'natural disasters'. Suffering and tragedy have always led to the question 'Why me?' The random nature of human suffering leads many to question the existence of a loving God. What Jesus makes clear in the first part of this gospel passage is that suffering is not necessarily brought about by sin. Those who suffered at the hands of Pilate and in the collapse of the tower of Siloam were no guiltier than their fellows. Jesus does not explain at this point the meaning of innocent suffering. He acknowledges that it is part of the human condition. The answer he will give will be seen on Calvary.

The second part of the gospel reading contains the parable of the fig tree. Whereas in the gospels of Matthew and Mark, Jesus is seen cursing the fig tree which carries no fruit (Mark chapter 11 and Matthew chapter 21), here in Luke Jesus uses a parable to make the same point. The fig tree symbolises the people and their lack of fruitfulness. The gardener 'intercedes' for the fig tree, recalling the role of Jesus in relation to sinners. The gardener makes his appeal, but we are not told the reply. We may presume that the fig tree was granted a reprieve, but for how many years?

*How long do I wait before responding to the call of God, the call of conscience?*

*What consolation can a Christian offer in the face of innocent suffering?*
*We pray for openness to learn from the words of Christ.*
*We pray for generosity in living out the gospel.*

---

# Fourth Sunday of Lent (Year C)

## Luke 15:1–3, 11–32

The tax collectors and sinners, however, were all crowding round to listen to him, and the Pharisees and scribes complained saying, 'This man welcomes sinners and eats with them.' So he told them this parable.

'There was a man who had two sons. The younger one said to his father, "Father, let me have the share of the estate that will come to me." So the father divided the property between them. A few days later, the younger son got together everything he had and left for a distant country where he squandered his money in loose living.

'When he had spent it all, that country experienced a severe famine, and now he began to be in need; so he hired himself out to one of the local inhabitants who sent him into the fields to feed the pigs. And he would willingly have filled himself with the pods which the pigs were eating, but no one would let him have them. Then he came to his senses and said, "How many of my father's hired men have all the food they want and more, and here am I dying of hunger! I will get up and go to my father and say: Father, I have sinned against heaven and against you; I no longer deserve to be called your son; treat me as one of your hired men." So he got up and went back to his father.

'While he was still a long way off, his father saw him and was moved with pity. He ran to the boy, clasped him in his arms and kissed him. Then his son said, "Father, I have sinned against heaven and against you. I no longer deserve to be called your son." But the father said to his servants, "Quick! Bring out the best robe and put it on him; put a ring on his finger and sandals on his feet. Bring the fattened calf, and kill it; we will celebrate by having a feast, because this son of mine was dead and has come back to life; he was lost and is found." And they began to celebrate.

'Now the elder son was out in the fields, and on his way back, as he drew near the house, he heard music and dancing. Calling one of the servants he asked what it was all about. The servant told him, "Your brother has come, and your father has killed the fattened calf because he has got him back safe and sound." He was angry then and refused to go in, and his father came out and began to plead with him; but he retorted to his father, "Look! All these years I have slaved for you and never disobeyed your orders, yet you never gave me so much as a young goat for me to celebrate with my friends. But, for this son of yours, when he comes back after swallowing up your property with prostitutes you kill the fattened calf." Then the father said, "My son, you are with me always and all I have is yours. But it was only right we should celebrate and rejoice, because your brother here was dead and has come to life; he was lost and is found."'

**Other readings: Joshua 5:9–12   Psalm 33 (34)   2 Corinthians 5:17–21**

The father welcomes back the return of his younger son with great extravagance. Nothing is too much to offer. Such is God's delight at the return of a sinner.

The contrasting attitude of the elder son is the main message of the parable, which is told for those who contest Jesus' welcoming attitude to sinners (15:1–3). Perhaps the elder son has a reasonable grievance. Did the father never show gratitude to him for his commitment, his 'slaving'? The words of the father to this elder son are truly healing words: 'My son, you are with me always and all I have is yours.'

*Do I have a welcoming attitude to those who seek God after going astray?*
*Would I, like the elder son, refuse to go in?*
*We pray for generous appreciation of the commitment of others.*
*We pray that we may have the humility to change our ways.*

# *Fifth Sunday of Lent (Year C)*

## *John 8:1–11*

Jesus went to the Mount of Olives.

At daybreak he appeared in the Temple again; and the whole people came to him, and he sat down and began to teach them. The scribes and Pharisees brought a woman who had been caught in adultery; and making her stand there in the middle they said to Jesus, 'Teacher, this woman has been caught in the very act of committing adultery. In the Law Moses ordered us to stone women of this kind. What do you say?' This they said testing him, so that they might have an accusation to bring against him. But Jesus bent down and started writing on the ground with his finger. When they kept on questioning him, he straightened up and said, 'Let the one among you who is without sin be the first to throw a stone at her.' Then bending down again he continued writing on the ground. When they heard this they went away one by one, beginning with the eldest, until the last one had gone and Jesus was left alone with the woman, standing in the middle. Then Jesus straightened up and said to her, 'Woman, where are they? Has no one condemned you?' She replied, 'No one, sir.' Then Jesus said, 'Neither do I condemn you. Go! And from now on do not sin again.'

**Other readings: Isaiah 43:16–21   Psalm 125 (126)   Philippians 3:8–14**

HAVING HAD GOSPEL READINGS from Luke for many Sundays now, we might be surprised that this Sunday gospel is from the Gospel of John. All is not as it seems. This gospel story, although found in John, is very similar to stories in the synoptic gospels of Matthew, Mark and Luke. It is absent from some ancient copies of John, and has long been considered an insertion into John's gospel. It is, nevertheless, reliable gospel tradition, but comes from an unknown source. The early Christians deliberately put down in writing all the traditions about Jesus they had received.

The theme of forgiveness is prominent, as on previous Sundays. Jesus is being tested, as so often by the religious leaders of his day. The matter of fidelity to the Law of Moses is raised in a dramatic way.

The actions of Jesus are eloquent. He crouches down to write on the ground, turning away from judgement and condemnation. He then 'straightens up' to deliver words of forgiveness, words which restore her life to the woman and allow her to rise up. Words of forgiveness empower us to stand erect, and to accept the challenge not to sin again.

*Am I prepared to understand and pardon the sinner?*
*Do I value the Sacrament of Reconciliation as a way of receiving for myself the new future offered to the woman in the gospel passage?*
*We pray for readiness to seek the forgiveness of Christ.*
*We pray for all those trapped in lives of abuse.*

---

# *Passion (Palm) Sunday (Year C)*

## *Luke 22:14 – 23:56*

When the time came he took his place at table, and the apostles with him. And he said to them, 'I have ardently longed to eat this Passover with you before I suffer; because, I tell you, I shall not eat it until it is fulfilled in the kingdom of God.' Then, taking a cup, he gave thanks and said, 'Take this and share it among you, because from now on, I tell you, I shall never again drink from the fruit of the vine until the kingdom of God comes.'

Then he took bread, and when he had given thanks, he broke it and gave it to them, saying, 'This is my body given for you; do this in remembrance of me.' And the cup similarly after supper saying, 'This cup is the new covenant in my blood, poured out for you.

'But look, here with me on the table is the hand of the man who is betraying me. The Son of man is indeed going as it is decreed, only alas for that man by whom he is betrayed!' And they began to question one another which of them it could be who intended to do this.

An argument also began between them about who of them should be reckoned the greatest; but he said to them, 'The kings of the gentiles lord it over them, and those who have authority over them are given the title Benefactor. Not so with you, but the greatest among you must be as the youngest, the leader as the one who serves. For who is the greater: the one at table or the one who serves? The one at table, surely? Yet I am among you as one who serves!

'You are those who have endured with me in my trials; and now I confer a kingdom on you, just as my Father conferred one on me. You may eat and drink at my table in my kingdom, and you will sit on thrones judging the twelve tribes of Israel.

'Simon, Simon! Look, Satan has been granted to sift you all like wheat; but I have prayed for you, Simon, that your faith may not fail; and sometime you must turn back and strengthen your brothers.' He answered, 'Lord, with you I am ready to go to prison and to death.' Jesus replied, 'I tell you, Peter, the cock will not crow today before you have denied three times that you know me.'

He said to them, 'When I sent you out without purse or bag or sandals, were you short of anything?' They answered, 'Nothing.' He said to them, 'But now anyone who has a purse, should take it, and the same with a bag; anyone who has no sword, should sell his tunic and buy one, for I say to you that this scripture must be fulfilled in me, *He was reckoned as one of the lawless*. And indeed what is written about me is being fulfilled.' They said, 'Lord, here are two swords.' He said to them, 'That is enough!'

He then left to make his way as usual to the Mount of Olives, with the disciples following. When he reached the place he said to them, 'Pray that you do not enter into temptation.'

Then he withdrew from them, about a stone's throw, and knelt down and prayed, saying, 'Father, if you are willing, take this cup away from me. Yet not my will but yours be done.' Then an angel from heaven appeared to him, strengthening him. In his anguish he prayed more earnestly, and his sweat became like drops of blood falling to the ground. Standing up from prayer and going to the disciples he found them sleeping from grief. And he said to them,

'Why are you asleep? Get up and pray that you do not enter into temptation.'

While he was still speaking, a crowd suddenly appeared, and the one called Judas, one of the Twelve, was leading them. And he approached Jesus to kiss him. Jesus said, 'Judas, are you betraying the Son of man with a kiss?' Those around him, seeing what was going to happen, said, 'Lord, shall we strike with the sword?' And one of them struck the high priest's servant and cut off his right ear. But at this Jesus said, 'Leave it at that!' And touching his ear he healed him.

Then Jesus said to the chief priests and officers of the guard and elders who had come for him, 'Have you come with swords and clubs as though I were a bandit? When I was with you in the Temple day by day you did not lift a hand against me. But this is your hour and the reign of darkness.'

They seized him then and led him away, and they took him into the high priest's house. Peter followed at a distance. When they had lit a fire in the middle of the courtyard and had sat down together, Peter sat down among them, and a servant-girl, seeing him sitting in the light, peered at him, and said, 'This man was with him too.' But he denied it saying. 'I do not know him, woman.' Shortly afterwards someone else saw him and said, 'You are one of them too.' But Peter replied, 'Man, I am not.' A little later another person saw him and insisted, 'For certain this man was with him also, for he is a Galilean too.' Peter said, 'Man, I do not know what you are talking about.' And immediately, while he was still speaking, the cock crowed, and the Lord turned and looked straight at Peter, and Peter remembered the Lord's words when he had said to him, 'Before the cock crows today, you will deny me three times.' And he went outside and wept bitterly. Meanwhile the men who were holding Jesus were mocking and beating him. They blindfolded him and questioned him, saying, 'Prophesy! Who hit you?' And they kept heaping many other insults on him.

When day broke a meeting of the elders of the people, the chief priests and scribes was convened, and they brought him before their council, saying, 'If you are the Messiah, tell us.' But he said to them, 'If I tell you, you will not believe, and if I question you, you will not answer. But from now on, the *Son of man* will be *seated at the right hand* of the Power *of God.*' They all said, 'So you are the Son of God?' He answered, 'You say that I am.' Then they said, 'Why do we still need any evidence? We have heard it ourselves from his own lips.' The whole gathering then rose and brought him before Pilate.

They began to accuse him, saying, 'We found this man inciting our people to revolt, forbidding payment of taxes to Caesar, and claiming to be the Messiah, a king.' Pilate asked him, 'Are you the king of the Jews?' He replied, 'You say so.' Pilate then said to the chief priests and the crowds, 'I find no case against this man.' But they insisted, 'He is stirring up the people, teaching all over Judaea and starting from Galilee all the way to this place.' Hearing this, Pilate asked if the man were a Galilean; and having discovered that he came under Herod's jurisdiction, he sent him off to Herod, who was also in Jerusalem at that time.

Herod was delighted to see Jesus; he had been wanting for a long time to set eyes on him; moreover, he was hoping to see some sign done by him. So he questioned him at some length, but without getting any reply. Meanwhile the chief priests and the scribes were there, vehemently pressing their accusations. Then Herod, together with his guards, treated him with contempt and made fun of him; he put a rich cloak on him and sent him back to Pilate. And Herod and Pilate became friends that day, though formerly they had been at enmity with each other.

Pilate then summoned the chief priests and the leading men and the people, and said to them, 'You brought this man before me as inciting the people to revolt. See, I have examined him in your presence and found no case against this man in any of the charges you bring against him. Neither has Herod, since he has sent him back to us. See, he has done nothing that deserves death, so I shall have him beaten and release him.' But as one man they all howled, 'Take this man away! Release Barabbas for us!'(This man had been thrown into prison because of a riot in the city and murder.)

Again Pilate addressed them, wanting to release Jesus again, but they swelled their shouting, 'Crucify! Crucify him!' And for a third time he spoke to them, 'But what evil has this man done? I have found no case against him that deserves death, so I shall have him beaten and release him.' But they insisted, demanding at the top of their voices, that he should be crucified. And their voices prevailed.

Pilate then gave his verdict, that their demand was to be granted. He released the man they asked for, who had been imprisoned for riot and murder, and handed Jesus over to them as they wished.

As they were leading him away they seized on a man, Simon from Cyrene, who was coming from the country, and laid on him the cross to carry behind Jesus. A large number of the people followed him, and women, who beat their breasts and mourned for him. But Jesus turned to them and said, 'Daughters of Jerusalem, do not weep for me; but weep for yourselves and for your children. For look, the days are coming when people will say, "Blessed are the barren, the wombs that have not borne children, the breasts that have not given suck!" Then they will begin to *say to the mountains, "Fall on us!" and to the hills, "Cover us!"* For if they do this when the wood is green, what will they do when it is dry?' Two others also, criminals, were led out to be put to death with him.

When they reached the place called The Skull, there they crucified him and the criminals, one on his right, the other on his left. Jesus said, 'Father, forgive them; for they do not know what they are doing.' Then they cast lots to share out his clothing. The people stood watching. As for the leaders, they scoffed at him saying, 'He saved others, let him save himself if he is the Messiah of God, the Chosen One.' The soldiers mocked him too, coming up to him, offering him vinegar, and saying, 'If you are the king of the Jews, save yourself.' There was also an inscription over him: 'This is the King of the Jews'.

One of the criminals hanging there jeered at him: 'Are you not the Messiah? Save yourself and us.' But in reply the other rebuked him saying. 'Do you not fear God, since you are under the same sentence? And we justly, for we are getting what we deserve for what we did. But this man did nothing wrong.' Then he said, 'Jesus, remember me when you come into your kingdom.' He answered him, 'Amen I say to you, today you will be with me in paradise.'

It was now about noon and darkness came over the whole land until mid-afternoon, as the sun's light failed. The curtain of the Temple was torn right down the middle. Jesus cried out in a loud voice saying, 'Father, *into your hands I commit my spirit.*' Having said this, he breathed his last. When the centurion saw what had taken place, he gave glory to God and said, 'Truly, this was a just man.' And when all the crowds who had gathered for the spectacle saw what had happened, they went home beating their breasts. All his friends stood at a distance, and also the women who had followed with him from Galilee, watching these things.

Now a man named Joseph, a member of the council, a good and righteous man, had not agreed with their plan and their action. He came from Arimathaea, a Jewish town, and was awaiting the kingdom of God. This man approached Pilate and asked for the body of Jesus. Then he took it down, wrapped it in a linen cloth and laid it in a rock-hewn tomb in which no one had ever yet been laid. It was the day of preparation and the Sabbath was beginning to grow light. The women who had come from Galilee with Jesus followed behind and saw the tomb and how the body had been laid. They went back and prepared spices and ointments. And on the Sabbath day they rested, in accordance with the commandment.

**Other readings: Isaiah 50:4–7   Psalm 21 (22)   Philippians 2:6–11**

EVEN AMID SUFFERING JESUS shows great compassion to others. He prays for forgiveness for his executioners, who 'do not know what they are doing'. He promises paradise to the criminal who seeks forgiveness.

Jesus' final words in Luke are taken from Psalm 31, 'Into your hands I commit my spirit.' The evangelist tells us of the trust of Jesus at the moment of death. Jesus knows that the Father will not abandon him, but raise him up on the third day. As the story of Jesus' death concludes, the hope of resurrection remains.

# PASSION (PALM) SUNDAY (YEAR C)

*What are the striking features of the story of the Passion as told by Luke?*

*Take time this week to read the complete story of the Passion and death of Christ.*

*We pray for the willingness to die with Christ in order to rise with him to new life.*

*Let us join with the Church throughout the world to live Holy Week to the full.*

# EASTER

## *Easter Sunday*

### *John 20:1–9*
Early on the first day of the week when it was still dark, Mary of Magdala came to the tomb. She saw that the stone had been moved away from the tomb and came running to Simon Peter and the other disciple, the one whom Jesus loved, and said to them, 'They have taken the Lord out of the tomb, and we do not know where they have put him.'

So Peter set out with the other disciple to go to the tomb. The two ran together, but the other disciple, running faster than Peter, reached the tomb first; he bent down and saw the linen cloths lying there, but did not go in. Simon Peter, following him, also came up, went into the tomb, saw the linen cloths lying there and also the cloth that had been on his head; this was not with the linen cloths but rolled up in a place by itself. Then the other disciple who had reached the tomb first also went in; he saw and he believed. Till this moment they had still not understood the scripture, that he must rise from the dead.

Other readings: Acts 10:34, 37–43   Psalm 117 (118)   Colossians 3:1–4

EACH ONE OF OUR four canonical gospels ends with stories of the discovery of the empty tomb and accounts of appearances of the risen Jesus. Throughout the first week of the Easter period the gospel at Mass is taken from this material. Today we read John's account of the discovery of the empty tomb. The account gives a prominent role to Mary Magdalene, who becomes known by Christians as 'the apostle to the apostles'. It is she who discovers the empty tomb and passes on the news. Why is it empty? She will know why when Jesus appears to her later in the chapter.

The disciple whom Jesus loves, thought to be the author of the account, is convinced of the resurrection without even seeing the risen Jesus. It is sufficient for him to see that the body of Jesus no longer lies in the tomb. The later appearance of Jesus to the eleven disciples will confirm what he already knows.

Christian faith proclaims: 'Christ has died! Christ is risen! Christ will come again!' Without the resurrection, the real rising of Jesus to new life in a transformed and glorified body, there would be no good news to proclaim. The God of love is more powerful than death and sin, and God has shown this in raising Jesus, who became a victim of sin, to the life of the resurrection. The world is in dire need of news that is true, amid so many messages which are false, undermining and deceptive. True hope lies in the God who raised Jesus from the dead.

*Do I appreciate the fundamental significance of the resurrection of Jesus?*
*Do I have the vision to see the wonders God works in each human life?*
*We pray for those baptised and those received into the Catholic Church this Easter.*
*We pray for Christians for whom the cross is a daily and painful reality, that they will know that the risen Christ is at their side.*

---

# YEAR A

## Second Sunday of Easter (Year A)

### John 20:19–31

In the evening of that same day, the first day of the week, the doors were closed in the room where the disciples were, for fear of the Jews. Jesus came and stood among them and said to them, 'Peace be with you,' and, after saying this, he showed them his hands and his side. The disciples rejoiced at seeing the Lord, and he said to them again, 'Peace be with you.

'As the Father has sent me,
so am I sending you.'

After saying this he breathed on them and said:

'Receive the Holy Spirit.
If you forgive anyone's sins,
they are forgiven;
if you retain anyone's sins,
they are retained.'

Thomas, called the Twin, who was one of the Twelve, was not with them when Jesus came. So the other disciples said to him, 'We have seen the Lord,' but he answered, 'Unless I see in his hands the mark of the nails and put my finger in the mark of the nails, and my hand into his side, I will not believe.' Eight days later the disciples were in the house again and Thomas was with them. Although the doors were closed, Jesus came and stood among them and said, 'Peace be with you.' Then he said to Thomas, 'Put your finger here, and see my hands. Reach out your hand and put it in my side. Do not doubt but believe.' Thomas replied, 'My Lord and my God!' Jesus said to him:

'Do you believe because you have seen me?
Blessed are those who have not seen and yet have come to believe.'

Jesus did many other signs in the sight of the disciples, which are not written in this book. These are written so that you may believe that Jesus is the Christ, the Son of God, and that by believing you may have life in his name.

**Other readings: Acts 2:42–47  Psalm 117 (118)  1 Peter 1:3–9**

THE GOSPEL OF JOHN provides an account of the appearance of Jesus to the eleven in the upper room and a second account one week later (eight days in Hebrew reckoning). Jesus brings the gift of peace and the gift of the Holy Spirit for the forgiveness of sins. Jesus, who has died for sinners, ensures the gift of forgiveness for all those who will seek it, the forgiveness available to us through the Sacrament of Reconciliation.

The reluctance of Thomas provokes Jesus' praise for those who believe without seeing. But Thomas should also be remembered as the one who gives the fullest declaration of faith in Christ found anywhere in the gospels: 'My Lord and my God!'

*Do I treasure the gospel as showing the way to faith and life?*
*How does the experience of Thomas provide encouragement for believers?*
*We pray for a deeper appreciation of the Sacrament of Reconciliation.*
*We pray for all those plagued by hesitation and doubt.*

---

# Third Sunday of Easter (Year A)

## Luke 24:13-35

Now that same day, two of them were on their way to a village called Emmaus, twelve kilometres from Jerusalem, and they were talking together about all that had happened. And it happened that as they were talking together and discussing it, Jesus himself came near and was walking with them; but their eyes were prevented from recognising him. He said to them, 'What are you discussing as you walk along?' And they stood still, their faces downcast.

Then one of them, called Cleopas, answered him, 'Are you the only stranger in Jerusalem who does not know what has been happening there these last few days.' He asked, 'What sort of things?' They answered, 'About Jesus of Nazareth, who showed himself a prophet powerful in action and speech before God and the whole people; how our chief priests and leaders handed him over to be sentenced to death, and crucified him. We had hoped that he was the one to set Israel free. But besides all this, it is now the third day since all this happened; and some women from our group have astounded us: they went to the tomb in the early morning, and when they could not find the body, they came back to tell us they had seen a vision of angels who said that he was alive. Some of those with us went to the tomb, and found everything exactly as the women had reported, but of him they saw nothing.' Then he said to them, 'How foolish you are! So slow to believe all that the prophets said! Was it not necessary that the Messiah should suffer and so enter into his glory?' Then, starting from Moses and from all the prophets, he explained to them the passages about himself throughout the scriptures.

When they drew near to the village to which they were

going, he himself made as if to go on; but they pressed him, saying, 'Stay with us! It is towards evening, and the day is almost over.' So he went in to stay with them. Now while he was with them at table, he took the bread and said the blessing; then he broke it and handed it to them. And their eyes were opened and they recognised him; but he had vanished from their sight. Then they said to each other, 'Were not our hearts burning within us as he talked to us on the road and opened the scriptures to us?'

They got up that same hour and returned to Jerusalem. There they found the Eleven assembled together with their companions, who said to them, 'The Lord has indeed risen and has appeared to Simon.' Then they recounted what had happened on the road and how they had recognised him at the breaking of bread.

**Other readings: Acts 2:14, 22–33   Psalm 15 (16)   1 Peter 1:17–21**

THE STORY OF THE two disciples on the road to Emmaus is perhaps the most endearing of the Easter appearances. The Risen Jesus brings new hope to two men who have lost all hope. He feeds their minds and their hearts by explaining the Scriptures to them. His true identity is revealed in the bread he breaks for them. Their experience is offered to us too at every Eucharist, as we receive the Word and the Sacrament and are strengthened in holiness.

*Do our hearts burn within us as we are nourished by the Scriptures?*
*What can we do to ensure this is so?*
*We pray for a deeper appreciation of the gift of the Eucharist.*
*May the hope brought by the Risen Christ truly transform us.*

---

# *Fourth Sunday of Easter (Year A)*

## *John 10:1–10*

Jesus said: 'Amen, Amen I say to you, anyone who does not enter the sheepfold through the gate, but climbs in some other way, is a thief and a bandit. He who enters through the gate is the shepherd of the flock; to him the gatekeeper opens the gate, the sheep hear his voice, he calls his own sheep by name and leads them out. When he has brought out all his sheep, he goes ahead of them, and the sheep follow because they know his voice. They will never follow a stranger, but will run away from him because they do not recognise the voice of strangers.'

Jesus told them this parable but they failed to understand what he was saying to them.

So Jesus spoke to them again:

'Amen, Amen I say to you,
I am the gate for the sheep.
All who have come before me
are thieves and bandits,
but the sheep did not listen to them.
I am the gate.
Anyone who enters through me will be safe,
and will go in and out
and will find pasture.
The thief comes
only to steal and kill and destroy.
I have come
so that they may have life
and have it in plenty.'

**Other readings: Acts 2:14, 36–41  Psalm 22 (23)  1 Peter 2:20–25**

ON MOST OF THE days of the Easter season, which goes from Easter Sunday until Pentecost, the gospel passage set down to be read at Mass is from the Gospel of John. This gospel, also known as the Fourth Gospel, contains rich teaching and new understandings of Jesus which supplement what is found in the other gospels. Our reading this Sunday is from the tenth chapter of John, in which we are presented with the image of Jesus as the good shepherd.

In the verses read this year there is an additional focus. While Jesus contrasts the shepherd of the sheep with the 'thief' and the 'bandit', he goes on to refer to himself as 'the gate for the sheep'. Not only does Jesus lead his people, but he is also the way through which they enter to reach life. The Risen Lord is 'the way, the truth and the life' (John 14:6).

Jesus comes 'so that we may have life and have it in plenty' (verse 10). The Easter season is a prolonged celebration of the gift of life which we receive from the moment of Baptism, and the anticipation of our full sharing in it in the life to come.

The second reading also celebrates the new life of baptism. The image of the shepherd is found here too, as Jesus is called the 'shepherd and guardian of our souls'.

*How effective is the image of Jesus as the 'good shepherd'?*
*Does the evangelist's use of images confuse or enlighten you?*
*Pray Psalm 22 (23) and ask for a deeper awareness that 'the Lord is my shepherd'.*
*We support by our prayer all those called to priesthood and the religious life.*

---

## *Fifth Sunday of Easter (Year A)*

### *John 14:1–12*
Jesus said to his disciples:

'Do not let your hearts be troubled.
You trust in God, trust also in me.
In my Father's house
there are many places to live in;
otherwise would I have told you
that I am going to prepare a place for you?
And after I have gone and prepared you a place,
I shall return to take you to myself,
so that where I am you may be also.
You know the way to the place where I am going.'
Thomas said, 'Lord, we do not know where you are going; how can we know the way?' Jesus said to him:

'I am the Way; I am Truth and Life.
No one comes to the Father except through me.

If you know me, you will know my Father also.
From this moment you know him and have seen him.'

Philip said to him, 'Lord, show us the Father and it is enough for us.' Jesus said to him, 'Have I been with you so long, Philip, and you still do not know me?

'Anyone who has seen me has seen the Father,
How can you say, "Show us the Father"?
Do you not believe
that I am in the Father and the Father is in me?
The words that I speak to you I do not speak on my own account:
but the Father, dwelling in me, is doing his works.
You must believe me when I say
that I am in the Father and the Father is in me;
otherwise believe it on the evidence of these works.
Amen, Amen I say to you,
whoever believes in me
will also do the same works as I do myself,
and will do greater works than these,
because I am going to the Father.'

**Other readings: Acts 6:1–7  Psalm 32 (33)  1 Peter 2:4–9**

THE ACCOUNT OF THE last evening of Jesus with his disciples in the Gospel of John includes several speeches, punctuated from time to time by interventions of the disciples. It is most appropriate that these passages are read during the second half of the Easter season as we approach the feast of the Ascension and the return of Jesus to the Father. Jesus' first words in today's passage are words of reassurance which contrast strongly with his earlier prediction of Judas' betrayal and Peter's denial.

Thomas asks about the way to the place where Jesus is going. 'I am the Way, the Truth and the Life,' says Jesus. The words of Jesus in John's gospel constantly underline that in him truth and life are to be found. Philip, on the other hand, is impatient to see the Father. Jesus' reply echoes the constant teaching of this gospel that 'the only Son has made God known' (John 1:18). Both the answer to our searching and the satisfaction of our longing are found in Christ. To know Jesus is to know the Father. To see Jesus is to see the Father.

*Do I recognise Jesus as the Way or do I reduce him to a talented prophet and healer?*
*How often do I give in to despondency and anxiety?*
*Pray for a deeper faith in the person of Jesus, our Lord and our God.*
*Pray for confidence in the continuing presence of Jesus in his Church.*

---

## *Sixth Sunday of Easter (Year A)*

### *John 14:15-21*
Jesus said to his disciples:

'If you love me you will keep my commandments.
I shall ask the Father,
and he will give you another Paraclete
to be with you for ever,
the Spirit of truth
whom the world can never accept
since it neither sees nor knows him;
but you know him,
because he dwells with you, he will be in you.
I shall not leave you orphans;
I shall come to you.
In a short time the world will no longer see me;
but you will see me because I live
and you also will live.
On that day
you will know that I am in my Father
and you in me and I in you.
Whoever holds to my commandments and keeps them
is the one who loves me;
and whoever loves me will be loved by my Father,
and I shall love and reveal myself to that person.'

**Other readings: Acts 8:5-8,14-17  Psalm 65 (66)  1 Peter 3:15-18**

## SIXTH SUNDAY OF EASTER (YEAR A)

OUR READING FROM THE Gospel of John contains one of several references, in the speeches of Jesus on the night before he dies, to the Advocate, the Holy Spirit. These references to the Spirit prepare us to celebrate the feast of Pentecost, which concludes the Easter season. Only in the Fourth Gospel is the Spirit referred to as 'the Advocate', 'the Paraclete', 'the Spirit of truth'. Jesus stresses that the world of sin, opposed as it is to truth and goodness, does not welcome the Spirit. In fact, the world of sin is incapable of receiving the Spirit.

Later in these speeches Jesus affirms that the Spirit will remind the disciples of what he has taught (14:26), and lead them into the fulness of truth (16:13).

Jesus reassures the disciples that he will not abandon them. Even though he will no longer be seen by the world, the bond between Jesus and his disciples endures. This bond is maintained by the Spirit. This bond is the life which Jesus shares with us, a bond which draws us deeper into the life of God.

This passage both begins and ends with reference to the commandments of Jesus. Living the commandments is proof of the love the disciples have for him. Jesus speaks later of his one commandment, 'love one another as I have loved you' (15:12). This Spirit-inspired love, shown in living the commandments and loving the brothers and sisters, keeps us fully alive in the new life of the Risen Jesus, drawing us deeper into the life of the Father.

These precious words of Jesus are like a symphony in which the different themes are played and played again in their various forms. The words of Jesus, with the Eucharist and the priesthood, are treasured parting gifts of the Lord to his friends, gifts which maintain his presence in a troubled and unbelieving world.

*Which of these words of Jesus speak to you most powerfully?*
*How might you be more prepared to receive the Spirit of truth?*
*Pray that you may experience the bond every disciple has with Father, Son and Holy Spirit.*
*Pray for all those who seek to bring God's love to a suffering world.*

# The Ascension of the Lord (Year A)

## Matthew 28:16-20

Now the eleven disciples set out for Galilee, to the mountain to which Jesus had directed them. When they saw him they worshipped him, though some hesitated. Jesus came up and spoke to them. He said, 'All authority in heaven and on earth has been given to me. Go, therefore, make disciples of all nations; baptise them in the name of the Father and of the Son and of the Holy Spirit, and teach them to observe everything I have commanded you. And look, I am with you always till the end of time.'

**Other readings: Acts 1:1-11   Psalm 46 (47)   Ephesians 1:17-23**

THIS GOSPEL READING CONTAINS the final verses of the Gospel of Matthew. There is no explicit reference to an ascension of Jesus, but this is the last meeting of Jesus with his disciples. The different gospels recount different appearances of the Risen Jesus. At the empty tomb the message had been given that Jesus was to go before them into Galilee. The only meeting of the Risen Lord with the eleven disciples in Matthew's gospel is this meeting on a mountain in Galilee. The gospel ends where the ministry of Jesus had begun, with his instructing the disciples on the mountain.

The initial encounter with Jesus is somewhat subdued. Matthew, like the other evangelists, reports a certain hesitation on the part of the eleven. There were some who hesitated. The gospel accounts speak of a transformation in the appearance of the Risen Jesus which may explain their hesitation. The disciples were not gullible individuals, desperate to continue their association with Jesus, but objective observers who wanted to make sense of what was happening.

The words of Jesus are solemn and forceful. He claims authority in a way he never did during his ministry. He sends the disciples forth to 'make disciples' of all the nations. The earlier hesitations in this gospel about preaching to non-Jews are put aside. Now is the time for a mission to the whole world.

The disciples are to baptise and to teach. Baptism is the sign of entry into the community of the disciples of Jesus, and of being drawn into the life of God, Father, Son and Holy Spirit. The reference to the Holy Trinity reflects the practice of the early Christians.

The final words of Jesus are an assurance of his continuing presence. The Gospel of Matthew began by explaining that the Saviour to be born is Emmanuel, 'God with us'. The Risen Lord now reassures the eleven that, despite his departure, he continues to be present with them, for he is with us always, until the end of time.

*What does the ascension of the Lord mean to you?*
*In what ways is Jesus present for us today?*
*Pray that we may never forget that Christ has taken our humanity with him to the Father.*
*Pray for the readiness to receive the Spirit of Jesus at Pentecost.*

---

# *Seventh Sunday of Easter (Year A)*

## *John 17:1-11*

After saying this, Jesus raised his eyes to heaven and said:

'Father, the hour has come:
glorify your Son
so that the Son may glorify you;
so that, just as you have given him
authority over all people,
he may give eternal life
to all those you have given to him.
And eternal life is this:
to know you,
the only true God,
and Jesus Christ whom you have sent.
I have glorified you on earth
by finishing the work that you gave me to do.
Now, Father, glorify me at your side
with that glory I had
before ever the world existed.
I have revealed your name
to those whom you gave me from the world.

# SEVENTH SUNDAY OF EASTER (YEAR A)

They were yours and you gave them to me,
and they have kept your word.
Now they know that all you have given me
comes from you,
for the words that you gave to me
I have given to them,
and they have indeed accepted them
and truly recognised that I came from you,
and have believed that it was you who sent me.
I am asking on their behalf;
I ask not on behalf of the world
but on behalf of those you have given me,
because they belong to you.
All I have is yours
and all you have is mine,
and in them I am glorified.
I am no longer in the world,
but they are in the world,
and I am coming to you.
Holy Father,
keep those you have given me true to your name,
so that they may be one as we are one.'

**Other readings: Acts 1:12-14  Psalm 26 (27)  1 Peter 4:13-16**

THESE ARE THE OPENING words of the prayer that the evangelist attributes to Jesus at the Last Supper, on the night before he died. Jesus speaks of the hour, towards which his whole life has been directed. Jesus prays that the Father will glorify him. This will happen through his death and resurrection, and the subsequent raising of Christ, with his risen humanity, to the presence of God. Through this Easter mystery eternal life is bestowed on those who believe.

The work of Jesus is now complete, and he prays for those who through his preaching have come to know the Father's name. He distinguishes them from the world which does not know or accept him. These true disciples have realized that Jesus comes from the Father and that his teaching is true and reliable.

Jesus stresses that his prayer is for those who believe and not for the world. While Jesus is soon to leave this world, his faithful followers will remain to continue his work. They will be supported by the prayer of Christ to the Father.

*What does Jesus mean when he says he is glorified?*
*How best can we hold firm to the teaching Jesus has given us?*
*Pray that the Church will be always aware of the prayer of Christ on our behalf.*
*Pray for strong faith which trusts that where Jesus has gone we too will follow.*

---

# YEAR B

## *Second Sunday of Easter (Year B)*

### *John 20:19-31*

In the evening of that same day, the first day of the week, the doors were closed in the room where the disciples were, for fear of the Jews. Jesus came and stood among them and said to them, 'Peace be with you,' and, after saying this, he showed them his hands and his side. The disciples rejoiced at seeing the Lord, and he said to them again, 'Peace be with you.

'As the Father has sent me,
so am I sending you.'

After saying this he breathed on them and said:

'Receive the Holy Spirit.
If you forgive anyone's sins,
they are forgiven;
if you retain anyone's sins,
they are retained.'

Thomas, called the Twin, who was one of the Twelve, was not with them when Jesus came. So the other disciples said to him,

# SECOND SUNDAY OF EASTER (YEAR B)

'We have seen the Lord,' but he answered, 'Unless I see in his hands the mark of the nails and put my finger in the mark of the nails, and my hand into his side, I will not believe.' Eight days later the disciples were in the house again and Thomas was with them. Although the doors were closed, Jesus came and stood among them and said, 'Peace be with you.' Then he said to Thomas, 'Put your finger here, and see my hands. Reach out your hand and put it in my side. Do not doubt but believe.' Thomas replied, 'My Lord and my God!' Jesus said to him:

'Do you believe because you have seen me?

Blessed are those who have not seen and yet have come to believe.'

Jesus did many other signs in the sight of the disciples, which are not written in this book. These are written so that you may believe that Jesus is the Christ, the Son of God, and that by believing you may have life in his name.

**Other readings: Acts 4:32-35  Psalm 117 (118)  1 John 5:1-6**

THE GOSPEL OF JOHN provides an account of the appearance of Jesus to the eleven in the upper room and a second account one week later (eight days in Hebrew reckoning). Jesus brings the gift of peace and the gift of the Holy Spirit for the forgiveness of sins. Jesus, who has died for sinners, ensures the gift of forgiveness for all those who will seek it, the forgiveness available to us through the Sacrament of Reconciliation.

The reluctance of Thomas provokes Jesus' praise for those who believe without seeing. But Thomas should also be remembered as the one who gives the fullest declaration of faith in Christ found anywhere in the gospels: 'My Lord and my God!'

*Do I treasure the gospel as showing the way to faith and life?*
*How does the experience of Thomas provide encouragement for*
    *believers?*
*We pray for a deeper appreciation of the Sacrament of Reconciliation.*
*We pray for all those plagued by hesitation and doubt.*

# Third Sunday of Easter (Year B)

## Luke 24:35–48

Then they recounted what had happened on the road and how they had recognised him at the breaking of bread.

They were still talking about all this when he himself stood among them and said to them, 'Peace be with you!' Staggered and frightened, they thought they were seeing a spirit. But he said, 'Why are you so agitated, and why are these misgivings rising in your hearts? See my hands and my feet, that it is I myself. Touch me and see for yourselves; a spirit does not have flesh and bones as you can see I have.' And as he said this he showed them his hands and his feet. As in their joy they still could not believe it, and were amazed, he said to them, 'Have you anything here to eat?' And they offered him a piece of grilled fish; he took it and ate it before their eyes.

Then he told them, 'This is what I said to you, while I was still with you, that everything written about me in the Law of Moses, in the Prophets and in the Psalms, must be fulfilled.' Then he opened their minds to understand the scriptures, and he said to them, 'It is written that in this way the Messiah should suffer and on the third day rise from the dead, and that, in his name, repentance for the forgiveness of sins should be preached to all nations, beginning from Jerusalem. You are witnesses to this.

**Other readings: Acts 3:13–15, 17–19  Psalm 4  1 John 2:1–5**

BEFORE IT CONCLUDES, THE Gospel of Luke gives us an account of the appearance of Jesus to the eleven in Jerusalem and his departure from them. The two disciples who had met Jesus on the road to Emmaus have given their report. Nevertheless, when Jesus appears, the disciples are still slow to believe. They were not gullible individuals, easily deceived. They struggle to comprehend what they are seeing.

Jesus demonstrates the reality of his risen body. Though transformed, he appears to them in bodily form. Jesus teaches them, as he taught the two disciples on the road, that the Scriptures can help them to grasp what has happened. The writings of the Law, Prophets and Psalms have been fulfilled. Israel's hopes and dreams of salvation have been realised. The challenge of faith invites all people to embrace a new life.

The disciples are sent out as witnesses to the world. The story of the spread of the gospel begins, and still continues today. The good news of Christ Risen must be told to all, beginning from Jerusalem and extending to the ends of the earth.

*Do I realise that faith is seeking to come to know the Risen Lord more fully day by day?*
*Do I strive for a love and deeper understanding of the Holy Scriptures?*
*Let us pray that the whole Church may be renewed in this Easter season.*
*Let us pray for the mission of the Church to the world of today.*

---

# *Fourth Sunday of Easter (Year B)*

## *John 10:11–18*
Jesus said:

'I am the good shepherd;
the good shepherd lays down his life for the sheep.
The hired man, since he is not the shepherd
and the sheep do not belong to him,
as soon as he sees a wolf coming,
abandons the sheep
and runs away,
and the wolf despoils and scatters the sheep;
because he is only a hired man
and has no concern for the sheep.
I am the good shepherd;
I know my own
and my own know me,
just as the Father knows me
and I know the Father.
And I lay down my life for my sheep.
And I have other sheep
that are not of this fold,
and I must lead these too.

# FOURTH SUNDAY OF EASTER (YEAR B)

They too will listen to my voice,
and there will be one flock,
one shepherd.
For this reason the Father loves me,
because I lay down my life
in order to take it up again.
No one takes it from me.
I lay it down of my own free will,
and I have power to lay it down,
and power to take it up again.
This command I received from my Father.'

**Other readings: Acts 4:8–12   Psalm 117 (118)   1 John 3:1–2**

THE DESCRIPTION OF JESUS as a shepherd adopts an image which is often used in the Hebrew Scriptures. The shepherds of Palestine provided for their sheep in so many varied ways that the image was used of the loving care of God for the people. In the Fourth Gospel the same image is elaborated in new ways.

Jesus is the good shepherd who gives his very life for his sheep. He contrasts his commitment to the sheep with the behaviour of the hired ones who flee at the first hint of danger. Jesus was fearless in the face of death in order to save his sheep.

Jesus knows the sheep. His knowledge of them, his familiarity with them as he enfolds them in his loving care, reflects the close relationship between the Father and the Son. The image of the shepherd is developed here with an extraordinary richness.

He will bring new members into his fold. The flock of Jesus Christ is not composed only of those who were first called. The mission of the followers of Jesus is limited by no boundaries of race, nation or origin. The unity of all the children of God is the goal of his coming and of his saving death and resurrection.

Our passage ends with a focus on the Lord's free and generous self-giving. In doing the Father's will he shows the power of his love, which is fully displayed in his rising to new life. The Good Shepherd is risen indeed, and shares his new life with us.

*Do I value my place in the flock of the good shepherd?*
*Do I do what I can to attract others to receive new life from the Risen Lord?*

*Let us pray for all pastors of the Church that they may truly imitate the Good Shepherd.*

*Let us pray that all those called to priesthood may respond with courage and generosity.*

---

## *Fifth Sunday of Easter (Year B)*

### John 15:1–8

Jesus said:

'I am the true vine,
and my Father is the vine-grower.
Every branch in me that bears no fruit
he cuts away,
and every branch that does bear fruit he prunes
to make it bear more fruit.
You are clean already,
through the word that I have spoken to you.
Remain in me, and I in you.
As a branch cannot bear fruit by itself,
unless it remains part of the vine,
neither can you unless you remain in me.
I am the vine,
you are the branches.
Whoever remains in me, and I in that person,
bears fruit in plenty;
for apart from me you can do nothing.
Anyone who does not remain in me
is thrown away like a branch and withers.
These branches are collected, thrown on the fire and burnt.
If you remain in me
and my words remain in you,
you may ask for whatever you please
and it will be done for you.
In this my Father is glorified,
that you should bear much fruit
and be my disciples.'

**Other readings: Acts 9:26–31  Psalm 21 (22)  1 John 3:18–24**

# FIFTH SUNDAY OF EASTER (YEAR B)

AS THE EASTER SEASON progresses our Sunday gospel readings are taken from the Gospel of John, which provides us with rich material for reflection on what Christ has done for us through his death and resurrection. We encounter this Sunday another image which Jesus uses to describe himself and his relationship with his disciples. Jesus is the true vine.

The symbol of the vine is found frequently in the Old Testament. The people of Israel are compared to a vine, which is supposed to bear abundant fruit. Jesus adopts the image to speak of the way in which he provides life for those who believe and follow him. He himself is the vine, and his followers are the branches. The process of growth and of bearing fruit is watched over by the Father, to whom the vine belongs.

The image of the vine is particularly effective because the branches cannot live without their attachment to the vine, neither can they be fruitful without the goodness provided by the vine. To live with Christ is to bear fruit. It is in drawing strength from Jesus that Christians can bear fruit in faith and good works.

The image also has its negative side. Branches which do not bear fruit are removed by the vine-grower and they are burnt. This development of the image invites us to consider the consequences of a refusal to be nourished by the kindness of God.

In the reading from the Acts of the Apostles we hear of Paul's attempts to join the Christian community after his conversion. It is only in connection with the people of Christ that we can truly be part of the vine. Through his resurrection Christ gives life to a new people.

*How can you derive more strength from the vine which is Christ?*
*How important do you consider it is to belong to the vine of Christ?*
*We pray for those who see faith as an individual pursuit.*
*We pray for a deeper sense of belonging in Christ.*

---

# Sixth Sunday of Easter (Year B)

## John 15:9–17
Jesus said:

'As the Father has loved me,
so have I loved you.

# SIXTH SUNDAY OF EASTER (YEAR B)

Remain in my love.
If you keep my commandments
you will remain in my love,
just as I have kept
my Father's commandments
and remain in his love.
I have told you this
so that my own joy may be in you
and your joy may be complete.
This is my commandment,
that you should love one another,
as I have loved you.
No one has greater love
than to lay down his life for his friends.
You are my friends,
if you do what I command you.
I shall no longer call you servants,
because the servant does not know
what the master is doing.
I call you friends,
because I have made known to you
everything I have heard from my Father.
You did not choose me,
but I chose you,
and I commissioned you
to go out and to bear fruit,
fruit that will last;
so that the Father will give you
whatever you ask him in my name.
These are my commands to you,
that you should love one another.'

**Other readings: Acts 10:25–26, 34–35, 44–48  Psalm 97 (98)  1 John 4:7–10**

THIS SUNDAY'S GOSPEL CONTINUES from the previous Sunday, when we heard Jesus describe himself as the true vine. We are listening to the farewell teaching of Jesus to his friends on the night before he died. There are several major themes here.

Jesus speaks of the love that the Father has for him. This same love he bestows on his disciples. If they are to remain in this bond of love they will keep his commandments, just as he keeps the commandments of the Father. Through discipleship they are bound not only to Jesus but also to the Father.

This belonging to the Son and to the Father is the cause of great joy, a joy shared by the Son and the disciples. Jesus foresees that the joy of the resurrection, the joy of seeing his triumph over sin and death, will abide with the disciples.

The love of which Jesus speaks is not simply love of God and love of neighbour, as in the other gospels, but love which imitates the love Jesus has shown, a love ready to lay down one's life for others, the love of the Good Shepherd defending his sheep.

The disciples are no longer considered servants, but friends. They are to know what Jesus has learnt from the Father. Being drawn closer to Christ means an increasing closeness to the Father. Jesus the master chooses his disciples. We are chosen and commissioned to go out and bear fruit. The image of the true vine and the branches bearing fruit, with which this chapter of the gospel began, returns.

*Does the love I show really reflect the self-giving love of Christ?*
*Have I really accepted that Jesus has chosen and commissioned me for a specific work?*
*We pray for those who see love as self-centred.*
*We pray for generosity and courage in our response to Christ.*

---

# *The Ascension of the Lord (Year B)*

## *Mark 16:15-20*

And he said to them, 'Go out to the whole world; proclaim the gospel to the whole creation. Whoever believes and is baptised will be saved; whoever does not believe will be condemned. These are the signs that will follow believers: in my name they will cast out demons; they will speak in new tongues; they will pick up snakes in their hands; should they drink deadly poison it will not harm them; they will lay their hands on the sick, who will recover.'

And the Lord Jesus, after he had spoken to them, was taken up into heaven; and sat down at the right hand of God,

# THE ASCENSION OF THE LORD (YEAR B)

while they, going out, proclaimed the good news everywhere, the Lord working with them and confirming the word by the signs that accompanied it.

**Other readings:** Acts 1:1-11  Psalm 46 (47)  Ephesians 4:1-13

ON THIS FEAST OF THE Ascension of the Lord we hear two accounts of the departure of Jesus. Our gospel reading gives the final verses of the Gospel of Mark. The eleven disciples are sent out by Jesus to the whole world and to preach to all creation. There is to be no limit to the delivery of the Christian good news. Those who accept the message with faith will receive salvation, and power to perform extraordinary signs. They will have the gift of healing, and they will be protected from all harm. The gospel concludes with the words that Jesus 'was taken up'.

The feast of the Ascension completes the mystery of the Resurrection by telling us that Jesus is now with the Father. He returns to the place from whence he came, but he returns with our humanity. Human nature sits in God's presence.

Our first reading, from the opening verses of the Acts of the Apostles, also tells of the ascension of the Lord. This version of the story includes Jesus' promise of the gift of the Holy Spirit, who will bring power from on high. This reading too speaks of the mission of the disciples: in Jerusalem, throughout Judaea and Samaria, and to the ends of the earth. The reading speaks of 'two men in white' who explain the departure of Jesus. This Jesus, who has gone to be with the Father, will return, they say, 'as you have seen him go'.

While the gospel reading stresses the gifts given to faith-filled disciples, our reading from Acts informs us that this power comes from the Holy Spirit, the Spirit received at Pentecost. It also encourages us to look to the return of Jesus. Christ has died! Christ is risen! Christ will come again!

*What does the feast of the Ascension say to all Christians?*
*Take note of how the two accounts of the Lord's departure complement each other.*
*We pray for an understanding of how deeply our humanity is valued by God.*
*We pray that we may treasure the humanity of all, particularly the poor and the lost.*

## *Seventh Sunday of Easter (Year B)*

### *John 17:11-19*

Jesus raised his eyes to heaven and said:

'Holy Father,
keep those you have given me true to your name,
so that they may be one as we are one.
While I was with them,
I kept those you had given me true to your name.
I have watched over them
and not one was lost
except one who was destined to be lost,
so that the scriptures might be fulfilled.
But now I am coming to you,
and I say these things in the world
so that they may have my joy completed in themselves.
I have given them your word,
and the world hated them,
because they do not belong to the world
just as I do not belong to the world.
I am asking you not to take them from the world,
but to protect them from the Evil One.
They do not belong to the world
just as I do not belong to the world.
Sanctify them in the truth;
your word is truth.
As you sent me into the world,
so I sent them into the world,
and for their sake I sanctify myself
so that they too may be sanctified in truth.'

**Other readings: Acts 1:15-17, 20-26   Psalm 102 (103)   1 John 4:11-16**

Chapter 17 of the Gospel of John contains a lengthy prayer of Jesus, set, just like the gospel readings of the previous two Sundays, in the context of the Last Supper. John's contribution to the gospel tradition here is unique.

This is a deep and intimate prayer, focused on the disciples, but also focused on us, as Jesus leaves us to return to the Father. Jesus prays that we be kept true to his name. It is easy to show enthusiasm at the beginning, but the life of faith has its good times and bad. Jesus speaks of the one who chose to be lost. The reference here is clearly to Judas, who freely turned against Jesus. God does not reject us, seeking the opportunity to condemn us. God yearns for our positive response of love. We can only lose ourselves.

Jesus is to leave this world, but he shares his joy with us, the joy of the resurrection which no one can take from us. But Jesus knows that the world is not a comfortable place for people of faith. We do not belong to the world, just as Jesus did not belong to the world. Nevertheless, he came into this world to bring freedom and truth. As Jesus goes to the Father, we are sure that through the Spirit, the Advocate, we can maintain our faith and consecration in the truth.

*What do I do to maintain my love for Jesus, and increase my understanding of his truth?*
*Do I allow the values of the world to deceive me so that I lose sight of the values given by faith?*
*Let us pray for those seeking direction and meaning in their lives, that they may be open to the guidance of the Holy Spirit.*
*We pray especially for those recently baptized and received into the Catholic Church, that they may persevere in fidelity to the truth revealed by Jesus.*

---

# YEAR C

## *Second Sunday of Easter (Year C)*

### John 20:19–31

In the evening of that same day, the first day of the week, the doors were closed in the room where the disciples were, for fear of the Jews. Jesus came and stood among them and said to them, 'Peace be with you,' and, after saying this, he showed them his hands and his side. The disciples rejoiced at seeing the Lord, and he said to them again, 'Peace be with you.

'As the Father has sent me,
so am I sending you.'

After saying this he breathed on them and said:

'Receive the Holy Spirit.
If you forgive anyone's sins,
they are forgiven;
if you retain anyone's sins,
they are retained.'

Thomas, called the Twin, who was one of the Twelve, was not with them when Jesus came. So the other disciples said to him, 'We have seen the Lord,' but he answered, 'Unless I see in his hands the mark of the nails and put my finger in the mark of the nails, and my hand into his side, I will not believe.' Eight days later the disciples were in the house again and Thomas was with them. Although the doors were closed, Jesus came and stood among them and said, 'Peace be with you.' Then he said to Thomas, 'Put your finger here, and see my hands. Reach out your hand and put it in my side. Do not doubt but believe.' Thomas replied, 'My Lord and my God!' Jesus said to him:

'Do you believe because you have seen me?

Blessed are those who have not seen and yet have come to believe.'

Jesus did many other signs in the sight of the disciples, which are not written in this book. These are written so that you may believe that Jesus is the Christ, the Son of God, and that by believing you may have life in his name.

**Other readings: Acts 5:12–16   Psalm 117 (118)   Apocalypse 1:9–13, 17–19**

THE GOSPEL OF JOHN provides an account of the appearance of Jesus to the eleven in the upper room and a second account one week later (eight days in Hebrew reckoning). Jesus brings the gift of peace and the gift of the Holy Spirit for the forgiveness of sins. Jesus, who has died for sinners, ensures the gift of forgiveness for all those who will seek it, the forgiveness available to us through the Sacrament of Reconciliation.

The reluctance of Thomas provokes Jesus' praise for those who believe without seeing. But Thomas should also be remembered as the one who gives the fullest declaration of faith in Christ found anywhere in the gospels: 'My Lord and my God!'

*Do I treasure the gospel as showing the way to faith and life?*
*How does the experience of Thomas provide encouragement for*
 *believers?*
*We pray for a deeper appreciation of the Sacrament of Reconciliation.*
*We pray for all those plagued by hesitation and doubt.*

## *Third Sunday of Easter (Year C)*

### *John 21:1-19*

After this, Jesus showed himself again to the disciples. It was by the Sea of Tiberias, and he showed himself in this way: Simon Peter, Thomas called the Twin, Nathanael from Cana in Galilee, the sons of Zebedee and two more of his disciples were together. Simon Peter said to them, 'I am going fishing.' They replied, 'We will come with you.' They went out and got into the boat but that night caught nothing.

When it was getting light, Jesus was standing on the shore, though the disciples did not know that it was Jesus. Jesus called out, 'Children, have you anything to eat?' They answered, 'No.' He said to them, 'Throw the net out to starboard and you will find something.' So they threw the net out and did not have strength to haul it in because of the number of fish. The disciple whom Jesus loved said to Peter, 'It is the Lord.' So Simon Peter, hearing that it was the Lord tied his outer garment round him (for he was stripped) and threw himself into the sea. The other disciples came on in the boat, towing the net with the fish; they were only about a hundred metres from land.

When they came ashore they saw a charcoal fire there with fish cooking on it and bread. Jesus said, 'Bring some of the fish you have just caught.' Simon Peter went aboard and dragged the net onto the shore, full of big fish, one hundred and fifty-three of them, and although there were so many the net was not broken. Jesus said to them, 'Come and have breakfast.' None of the disciples dared to ask him, 'Who are you?' knowing that it was the Lord. Jesus came, took the bread and gave it to them, and the same with the fish. This was the third time that Jesus showed himself to the disciples after being raised from the dead.

When they had finished breakfast, Jesus said to Simon Peter, 'Simon son of John, do you love me more than these?' He answered, 'Yes, Lord, you know that I love you.' Jesus said to him, 'Feed my lambs.' A second time he said to him, 'Simon son of John, do you love me?' He replied, 'Yes, Lord, you know that I love you.' Jesus said to him, 'Look after my sheep.' Then he said to him a third time, 'Simon son of John, do you love me?' Peter was hurt that he asked him a third time, 'Do you love me?' and said, 'Lord, you know everything; you know that I love you.' Jesus said to him, 'Feed my sheep.

'Amen, Amen I say to you,
when you were young
you put on your own belt and walked where you liked;
but when you grow old
you will stretch out your hands,
and someone else will put a belt round you
and take you where you would rather not go.'

He said this indicating by what sort of death he would glorify God. After this he said, 'Follow me.'

**Other readings: Acts 5:27-32, 40-41    Psalm 29 (30)    Apocalypse 5:11-14**

THIS IS THE ACCOUNT of the final appearance of Jesus to the disciples in the Gospel of John.

The scene is simple. The disciples seem disorientated, engaging in their previous occupation of fishing. Have they abandoned any idea of going out to preach the good news? The risen Jesus comes to them as a friend and provides for their needs: their need to make a living, their need for breakfast. The risen Christ retains his full humanity, including his concern for people in their day-to-day situations, however menial. The offering of bread and fish is a reminder of the miracle of the loaves and fishes worked in chapter 6 of the gospel, which pointed to the Eucharist, the memorial of his cross and resurrection to new life.

*Do I realise that in his resurrection Christ retains our humanity in all its ordinariness?*
*What does this appearance of Jesus teach us?*
*We pray for an appreciation of God's involvement in each present moment.*
*We pray for the courage to let the gospel live through our daily lives.*

---

# *Fourth Sunday of Easter (Year C)*

## *John 10:27–30*

Jesus said:

'My sheep listen to my voice;
I know them and they follow me.
I give them eternal life;
they will never be lost
and no one will ever snatch them from my hand.
What my Father has given me is greater than anything
and no one can snatch it from the Father's hand.
The Father and I are one.'

**Other readings: Acts 13:14, 43–52    Psalm 99 (100)**
**Apocalypse 7:9, 14–17**

HAVING LISTENED TO THE accounts of the appearances of the risen Jesus in the Gospel of John we now consider some of the words of Jesus from earlier in the gospel, which richly illustrate his mission and identity. We read from the Gospel of John throughout the Easter period due to its profound insights into the person and work of Jesus. It is most appropriate to reflect on these deep truths and rich images as we celebrate the resurrection of Jesus and his gift of new life to us.

Today's passage is taken from the tenth chapter of the gospel, which is renowned for Jesus' words: 'I am the good shepherd'. In fact, the chapter includes various sayings of Jesus relating to the image of the shepherd and his sheep. The use of this image, or parable, takes us back into the books of the Old Testament, where God is on several occasions described as a shepherd who has care for the sheep. The most famous instance of this is of course Psalm 22 (23), which begins with the words 'The Lord is my shepherd. There is nothing I shall want.'

Despite the brevity of today's passage from John's gospel, several important themes of the gospel occur. 'Belonging to Christ' as sheep to a shepherd presupposes hearing and accepting the word. In John's gospel we know Jesus himself as 'the Word'.

The gift of 'eternal life' is repeatedly promised in Jesus' teaching in this gospel. Christians are given a share in that life from the moment of baptism, and this is particularly underlined in John's gospel. The full realisation of this life will come in the life of the resurrection, but Jesus assures us that those who are members of the flock can never be lost.

Finally, Jesus speaks of his relationship with the Father. 'The Father and I are one' is a statement of enormous importance in helping us to understand the person of Jesus and the doctrine of the Holy Trinity.

*How do I respond to the call to follow Christ as my shepherd?*
*What consolation does this gospel passage provide?*
*We pray for a deeper sense of belonging to the world-wide 'flock of Christ'.*
*We pray for reverence and love for the mystery of God, who is Three in One.*

---

# Fifth Sunday of Easter (Year C)

## John 13:31–35

When Judas had gone out, Jesus said:

'Now has the Son of man been glorified,
and God has been glorified in him.

If God has been glorified in him,
God will glorify him in himself,
and will glorify him at once.
Little children,
yet a little while I am with you.
You will look for me,
and, as I told the Jews,
and I now say to you,
where I am going
you cannot come.
I give you a new commandment:
that you love one another;
you also must love one another
just as I have loved you.
By this everyone will know that
you are my disciples
if you have love for one another.'

**Other readings: Acts 14:21–27   Psalm 144 (145)   Apocalypse 21:1–5**

ONE OF THE PARTICULAR features of the Gospel of John is the discourse given by Jesus at the Last Supper. It is remarkable that five whole chapters of the gospel are dedicated to these words of Jesus, which are often referred to as the 'farewell discourse'. Along with other extensive teaching of Jesus in the Gospel of John, these speeches provide rich material for Christian reflection throughout the Easter period.

This passage is in two parts. Verses 31 and 32 follow on from the departure of Judas from the company of the disciples and of Jesus. John had written in verse 30: 'As soon as Judas had taken the piece of bread he went out. Night had fallen.' Judas departs into the night, where evil is plotted. By contrast, Jesus speaks of his glorification.

The word for 'glory', *doxa* in Greek, appears in the Prologue to John's gospel. Contemplating the whole mystery of the coming of the Son of God, the evangelist writes that 'we have seen his glory'. The 'glory' of Christ is the whole mystery by which he reveals the true nature of the Father, the true nature of God. This 'glory' is not fully revealed until the 'hour' of Jesus, the time of his cross and resurrection. In his death and resurrection the 'glory' of God, the self-giving, loving-kindness of God, is indeed revealed. Verse 31 uses words related to 'glory' on five occasions. The glory of the Son shows the glory of the Father.

Since we have been reborn in the death and resurrection of Christ, since we too have somehow 'seen his glory', then our lives are changed. We live according to the 'new commandment' Jesus speaks about in the second part of the gospel. The love we practise imitates the love of Christ, the love seen in the glory of his death and resurrection, a self-giving love which is lived out in daily commitment. Verses 34 to 35 contain four uses of the word 'love'. Through this love, 'everyone will know that you are my disciples'.

*What does the death and resurrection of Christ mean to me?*
*How can I imitate the love of Christ more fully?*
*We pray for a true understanding of the glory of Christ.*
*We pray that our example will draw others to Christ.*

---

# *Sixth Sunday of Easter (Year C)*

## *John 14:23–29*

Jesus said:

'Anyone who loves me will keep my word,
and will be loved by my Father,
and we shall come
and make a home in that person.
Anyone who does not love me does not keep my words.
And the word that you hear is not my own:
it is the word of the Father who sent me.
I have said these things to you
while I am still with you;
but the Paraclete, the Holy Spirit,
whom the Father will send in my name,
will teach you everything
and remind you of all I have said to you.
Peace I leave to you,
my own peace I give you,

# SIXTH SUNDAY OF EASTER (YEAR C)

not as the world gives do I give to you.
Do not let your hearts be troubled or afraid.
You heard me say:
I am going away and I am coming to you.
If you loved me you would be glad
that I am going to the Father,
for the Father is greater than I.
I have told you this now,
before it happens,
so that when it does happen
you may believe.'

**Other readings: Acts 15:1-2, 22-29   Psalm 66 (67)
Apocalypse 21:10-14, 22-23**

AS IN LAST WEEK'S gospel, we read this Sunday from the words of Jesus at the Last Supper in the Gospel of John, the so-called 'farewell discourse'. The theme of 'love' emerges again, not the love of one disciple for another, but the disciple's love for Jesus. Love for Jesus brings down the love of the Father. This love is shown by 'keeping the word' of Jesus, and keeping the word of Jesus is keeping the word of the Father who sent him. Jesus draws us into intimacy with the Father. What was stated in the very first chapter of the gospel is explained, that the only-begotten Son has made the unseen God known (1:18).

Fidelity to the word of Christ is not easy. Aware that the disciples will need assistance to recall and practise his word, Jesus promises that the Holy Spirit 'will teach you everything and remind you of all I have said'. To live as Christians requires this remembering of all that Jesus said and did, but also openness to the new insights provided by the Spirit, who is constantly active in the Church. The Spirit is given the name 'Paraclete', in Greek *parakletos*, which means one who is 'called alongside', one who is called to assist. John alone uses this term for the action of the Spirit.

The final verses speak of 'peace', the peace that the world cannot give. The departure of Jesus to the Father 'who is greater than I' should not undermine the peace of the disciples, for they already know the Father's closeness through Jesus.

*What does it mean to keep the word of Christ?*
*How do we know the closeness of the Father?*

*We pray for those who preach Christ's word.*
*We pray that we may be receptive to the work of the Spirit, called to assist us by Jesus.*

---

# *The Ascension of the Lord (Year C)*

### Luke 24:46–53

Jesus said to his disciples, 'It is written that in this way the Messiah should suffer and on the third day rise from the dead, and that, in his name, repentance for the forgiveness of sins should be preached to all nations, beginning from Jerusalem. You are witnesses to this. And see, I am sending upon you what the Father has promised. Stay in the city, then, until you have been clothed with power from on high.'

Then he took them out as far as Bethany, and raising his hands he blessed them. And it happened that as he blessed them, he withdrew from them and was carried up to heaven. They worshipped him and then went back to Jerusalem with great joy; and they were continually in the Temple praising God.

**Other readings: Acts 1:1–11    Psalm 46 (47)    Ephesians 1:17–23**

THIS GOSPEL READING CONTAINS the final verses of the Gospel of Luke. Each of the gospels comes to an end with the appearances of the risen Jesus. In Luke the climax comes with his appearance to the eleven disciples on the evening of the first day of the week, the same day on which the discovery of the empty tomb had been made.

Jesus declares that the Scriptures have been fulfilled in him. The events of his death and resurrection are the fulfilment of the hopes and expectations of Israel. The overriding theme here, however, is preparation for mission. The disciples will preach to all nations, beginning from Jerusalem. They are to be 'witnesses', the Greek word *martyres* reminding us that witness to Jesus can lead to death. The reading from the first chapter of the Acts of the Apostles makes the mission more explicit, saying that the disciples will preach 'not only in Jerusalem, but throughout Judaea and Samaria, and indeed to the ends of the earth'.

Once more there is the promise of the Holy Spirit, referred to here as 'power from on high'. The most remarkable manifestation of the Spirit will be on the day of Pentecost. The departure of Jesus here might seem like a rehearsal for the departure after forty days narrated in the Acts, that we recall and celebrate on this feast as the 'ascension' of the Lord. The important point is that, from the moment of his resurrection, Jesus is with the Father. The going up to heaven makes this point in graphic terms.

The gospel ends where it began, in the temple in Jerusalem. It began with Zechariah offering incense, and it ends with the disciples joyfully praising God. Despite the fact that Christ is no longer visible to us, we are filled with joy at his abiding presence.

*How do the Scriptures of the Old Testament prepare us for Christ?*
*What is the deep meaning of the ascension of the Lord?*
*Pray for the church scattered to 'the ends of the earth'.*
*Pray that we may joyfully receive 'power from on high' as we approach Pentecost.*

---

# *Seventh Sunday of Easter (Year C)*

## *John 17:20–26*
Jesus raised his eyes to heaven and said:

'Holy Father, I pray not only on behalf of these
but also on behalf of those
who through their teaching will come to believe in me,
that they may all be one,
just as, Father, you are in me and I am in you,
so that they also may be in us,
so that the world may believe that you sent me.
I have given them the glory
you have given to me,
that they may be one as we are one,
I in them and you in me,

that they may be perfected in unity
so that the world may know that it was you who sent me
and that you have loved them just as you have loved me.

'Father,
I want those you have given me
to be with me where I am,
so that they may always see my glory
which you have given me
because you loved me
before the foundation of the world.
Righteous Father,
the world has not known you,
but I have known you,
and these have known that you sent me.
I have made your name known to them
and will continue to make it known,
so that the love with which you loved me may be in them,
and so that I may be in them.'

**Other readings: Acts 7:55–60    Psalm 96 (97)
Apocalypse 22:12–14, 16–17, 20**

ON THIS SUNDAY BEFORE Pentecost we complete our readings from the words of Jesus in John's gospel set in the context of the Last Supper, on the night before Jesus died. This is the final section of a prayer Jesus directs to the Father. He raises his eyes to heaven and prays to the Father for unity.

Jesus prays not only for those who have followed him up to this point. He prays too for the people to whom they will bring the gospel message. Our awareness of the history of the early Church confirms that from the very start there were divisions and differences in attitudes which could be very strongly held.

Jesus prays for a pervasive unity among the disciples, that all may be one in a unity which reflects the relationship of Jesus with the Father, and the Trinitarian nature of God which is gradually being understood by the early Christians. Through this unity others will come to believe.

Jesus speaks of the glory given him by the Father which he in turn makes known to believers. Jesus has made the name of God, another word pointing to God's very essence, known to the disciples, so that they should be one in love. The ultimate gift of the Risen Jesus is love.

*How can these final words of Christ's prayer inspire our daily lives?*
*What can we do to protect the unity of those who believe and to avoid division and discord?*
*We pray that we may be faithful to the truth we have come to know from Jesus.*
*We pray that generous love may always be a feature of Christian life.*

---

## *Pentecost Sunday*

### *John 20:19–23*

In the evening of that same day, the first day of the week, the doors were closed in the room where the disciples were, for fear of the Jews. Jesus came and stood among them and said to them, 'Peace be with you,' and, after saying this, he showed them his hands and his side. The disciples rejoiced at seeing the Lord, and he said to them again, 'Peace be with you.

'As the Father has sent me,
so am I sending you.'

After saying this he breathed on them and said:

'Receive the Holy Spirit.
If you forgive anyone's sins,
they are forgiven;
if you retain anyone's sins,
they are retained.'

**Other readings: Acts 2:1–11    Psalm 103 (104)**
**1 Corinthians 12:3–7, 12–13[**

THIS GOSPEL READING FOR the feast of Pentecost has already been read, in a more extended form, on the Second Sunday of Easter.

It was read then to include Jesus' encounter with Thomas 'eight days later'. On the feast of Pentecost we have the opportunity to focus on the earlier verses, in which Jesus brings the gift of peace and the gift of the Holy Spirit.

The account of the day of Pentecost is found in our first reading, from the second chapter of the Acts of the Apostles. Fifty days after the resurrection there was a spectacular manifestation of the power of the Spirit. Jews and proselytes, gathered from the nations for the Jewish feast of Pentecost, witness the power of the Spirit and hear the preaching of the apostles each in his own tongue. This event launches the mission to the whole world.

Our gospel teaches that the Holy Spirit was also given by the risen Christ before the events of Pentecost. This is a quieter and more intimate demonstration of the power of the Spirit. It is related to the preaching of forgiveness and the possibility of new life for those who ask for it. The disciples are empowered to bring the forgiveness of Christ, but it is possible for people to reject this forgiveness. This seems to be the sense of the final verse, that some have their sins retained.

This is the final day of the Easter period. The Lord who died on the cross has shown himself in his risen body. He has taken our humanity into the presence of the Father. He is no longer visibly present, but his Spirit is with us to remind us of Jesus and to lead us into all truth. That Spirit, as St Paul writes to the Corinthians, bestows gifts in abundance for the benefit of the whole Church.

*Do I allow the Holy Spirit to transform my life?*
*Do I seek the peace and forgiveness offered to me through prayer and the sacraments?*
*Pray for the whole church, that Christians everywhere will be enlivened by the Holy Spirit.*
*Pray that the Easter gifts of Christ will always be with us.*